Gauriphanta Rd

Chauraha

Dudhwa

Escarpment Machan

Prince's Monsoon Machan

Tiger Copse

Jungle Pool

Twin Lakes

Junction Pool

Jungle Fowl Jetty

Leopard Bridge

Juliette Point

Croc Pool

TIGER HAVEN

Harriet's Silk Cotton Tree

Ghulli

D1604174

Nakauhwa

N

To Pallia

- Place
- - Park Boundary
✳ Rest House
✱ Machan

TIGER! TIGER!

by the same author

TIGER HAVEN
TARA: A TIGRESS
PRINCE OF CATS

TIGER!
TIGER!

Arjan Singh

JONATHAN CAPE
THIRTY BEDFORD SQUARE LONDON

First published 1984
Copyright © 1984 by Arjan Singh
Jonathan Cape Ltd, 30 Bedford Square, London WC1B 3EL

British Library Cataloguing in Publication Data

Singh, Arjan
Tiger! Tiger!
1. Tigers   2. Wildlife conservation – India
I. Title
639.9'7974428   QL737.C23

ISBN 0-224-02265-2

Printed in Great Britain by
Ebenezer Baylis & Son Ltd
The Trinity Press, Worcester and London

*To the tigers
of the
Dudhwa National Park*

Tiger! Tiger! burning bright
In the forest of the night,
What immortal hand or eye
Could frame thy fearful symmetry?

In what distant deeps or skies
Burned the fire of thine eyes?

WILLIAM BLAKE

CONTENTS

Contents

FOREWORD

The natural environment of most eminent conservationists is the committee room and the conference hall. Arjan Singh is only really at ease in the forests that surround his home, Tiger Haven, in the National Park that he virtually created, the Dudhwa, which will, I have no doubt, one day be named after him.

The author, whom I have known for many years, is quite unlike most other men. If one has to look for someone to compare him with, George Adamson springs to mind. Both are pioneer rehabilitators of great cats. Both prefer to work alone and both are highly subjective in the performance of their work. Arjan Singh has a deep physical love of his own wilderness, his own favourite species, the tiger, and certain individuals within that tribe. With George Schaller, whose work he admires, he shares a poetic quality in his approach to life and in his writings. This subjective romanticism, in my view, separates him from the bulk of ethologists whose painstaking observations, however fascinating to the specialist, are weighed down by an academic professionalism that bores the average reader and leaves him unmoved.

Tiger! Tiger! is an extraordinary book, for it reveals almost as much about the author as it does about the tiger itself. Regularly resurfacing as he writes is his passionate, even savage, commitment to preserve and protect his favourite beast. He who reads the book cannot fail to admire the author. It seems almost as if, having studied his hero so faithfully for so long, he has unwittingly grown like him. The nobility of the animal has washed off on the man.

The sadness here is that in spite of the value of his work and the virtue of his life, fame will come to him too late for him to be aware of it and, knowing him, all Arjan Singh would want of his own renown, posthumous or otherwise, would be to let it work to protect Tiger Haven, save Tara and her descendants, preserve the Dudhwa National Park and all its inhabitants, and save whatever can be saved of all the diminishing wilderness throughout the Earth.

JOHN ASPINALL

PREFACE

I have three reasons for presuming to write about tigers. The first is that, having grown up as a sport-killer, I have lived in tiger country, at peace with nature, for the past twenty-five years. For a quarter of a century I have devoted my life to the study of these marvellous animals. The hours I have spent tracking them, waiting for them, watching them and trying to photograph them are innumerable.

It was the American expert Chuck McDougal who remarked that when a man is looking for tigers in the jungle, they see him a hundred times for every time he sees one of them. This is undoubtedly true; and when I think of how often I must have passed close by them without knowing it, intruding on their territory, I can only marvel at their forbearance. I conclude that they have come to regard me in much the same light that I regard myself – as a kind of honorary tiger.

My second reason for writing about them is that I brought up Tara, a zoo-born tigress, in my house for seventeen months and returned her to the wild in an experiment prematurely condemned as impossible by people who called themselves wildlife experts. Far from being impossible, the venture proved an unqualified success. Having based herself on my home as she grew up, Tara went wild, mated with a wild tiger, and raised a family of three cubs, which are now over two years old. The experiment gave rise to furious controversy, which I shall describe in the course of this book. Suffice it to say that I have learnt an enormous amount from my association with Tara, during both her adolescence and her life as a wild tiger. No other human is likely to be as fortunate as I have been in opportunities for tiger study; and any lack of accurate observation or deduction, any failure of description, is due entirely to a lack of scientific training or literary ability on my part.

My third and last reason for writing is that I greatly fear that the enormous effort made by India to save the tiger from extinction is in danger of running aground on the rocks of prejudice and bureaucracy. Far too much emphasis is being placed on rigid scientific dogma, and not nearly enough on humanity and common sense. If the Project is to achieve lasting success, we must tackle its multifarious problems with open hearts, and learn the many lessons that nature has to teach us.

The eyes of the tiger are the brightest of any animal on earth. At dusk, or in the beam of a torch, they blaze back the ambient light with awe-inspiring intensity. It would be a tragedy, and a terrible dereliction of duty, if we allowed that magical fire to burn out.

I

THE MAN-EATER OF
BANGA JHALA

The forest hamlet of Garjia, on the west bank of the river Kosi, lies just outside the boundary of the Corbett National Park in Northern India. Across the river from Garjia, and connected to it by footpaths, are the village of Chopra and two others, all illegal encroachments into the forest made by villagers with the encouragement of unscrupulous local politicians. The area of wild, wooded country east of the river is known as Banga Jhala.

Short cuts between the hamlets, constantly used by villagers, run through forest of sal – a tall, straight-trunked hardwood tree – and lantana, an exotic plant first introduced to inhibit the growth of weeds, which it does effectively by covering large areas of ground. In fact it has spread so fast as to become a menace to forestry, but because it offers an ideal habitat for the tiger, it is a positive asset in wildlife areas. With the lantana, plenty of water, and a good supply of prey animals (chiefly sambar, chital and wild boar*), Banga Jhala is a perfect area for tigers – or would be, were it not for the human interlopers.

Late in the evening of March 21, 1979, two villagers who had been to collect their weekly rations in Garjia were returning

* A glossary of animal and bird names is given on pages 213 and 214.

13

home to Chopra with a pack-horse. Attracted by the animal's neighing, and disregarding the chatter of human voices which he had no doubt heard on numerous occasions as people passed through his domain, a tiger launched an attack on the horse as it came near a dense lantana thicket. It is not clear whether anyone was astride, but the tiger missed the horse, which bolted, and in the ensuing mêlée one of the men was knocked down and killed.

Since tigers do not normally prey on humans, whom they regard as an alien species, I presume that the attacker initially baulked at the strange carcass which he had got by accident, but that hunger and the confidence of being a big male then overcame his hesitation, and he had his first human meal.

Naturally the death created panic in the area; but as weeks went by with no further attack, fear gradually died down, and the incident was almost forgotten. Then, twenty-two months later, another man, also from Chopra, was taken – this time an employee of the forest department who set out alone as dawn was breaking on January 19, 1981 to mark stumps on a site where contractors were felling timber. This time the tiger made a deliberate kill though, once again, the exact circumstances of the attack are not known. It may be that the man had squatted down behind a bush to relieve himself, and that the tiger sprang on him in mistake for a four-legged animal. Six months later, on June 25, a third man, a lone honey collector, was also eaten, only fifty yards from where the second incident had taken place.

Pug-mark tracings confirmed that all three kills were the work of the same big male. Of course the blame for the deaths was placed on Project Tiger, the international scheme launched in 1972 by India and other nations for saving the tiger from extinction. Although the Corbett National Park had existed since 1935, new wildlife reserves had been created as part of the Project, and the population of tigers had stabilised, perhaps even increased. Now, people said, it was because their numbers had reached dangerous proportions that the man-eating had started. It was certainly true that tigers were living in the Banga Jhala buffer zone of forest outside the park.

The villagers went to their local politician, who happened to be a member of the National Government, and because he was a powerful man he was able to get the tiger officially declared a man-eater without delay. In other areas an attempt might well have been made to shoot the animal, but here C.B. Singh, the Field Director of the Park, had at least accepted my contention that alleged man-eaters should not be destroyed out of hand. He did not, however, agree with my suggestion that the tiger should be transferred to some more suitable area and given another chance there; rather, he planned, if he could catch it alive, to put it into a zoo.

His chances of capturing it intact would have been greatly improved if the Smithsonian Institution of Washington, D.C., had been allowed to carry out the survey of Indian tigers which they proposed at a meeting of the International Union for the Conservation of Nature at Delhi (I.U.C.N.) in 1969. The Smithsonian scientists – professionals at tranquillising and translocating wild animals – had planned to dart tigers and fit them with radio collars, to monitor their movements. Because the Indian Inspector-General of Forests and the Director of Project Tiger opposed the importation of telemetric equipment, the Americans transferred their project to Nepal, where they did excellent work in the Chitwan National Park.

Thus in 1981 India lacked both the equipment for darting tigers, and the experience of using it. The result was that when C.B. Singh and a young research assistant with no field experience set out to capture the man-eater of Banga Jhala, they were able to procure only one serviceable radio dart, and no antidote. Soon, after a fruitless wait for the tiger, they compounded their difficulties by irresponsibly firing off their single projectile at a female sambar, which fortunately they missed.

Their only hope now was to try to trap the tiger, and for this they got hold of a portable steel cage, which they camouflaged with vegetation and placed close to a site on which buffaloes had been tethered as baits. After the tiger had made a few kills, they laid a trail by dragging the remains of a dead bait to the cage and leaving it inside the drop-gate over the entrance. That night the tiger came, but after he had half-entered the cage he became alarmed and withdrew.

By then the operation had been made even more difficult by heavy monsoon rain. The river Kosi and all the local streams were in spate, and flood water lay everywhere. It was decided that if the next attempt failed, the whole campaign would have to be abandoned until the rains and floods had subsided. Another adverse factor was that the tiger had become exceedingly wary as a result of the continuous pursuit. Yet that very night, impelled by twenty-four hours of hunger, he sealed his own fate by stepping into the cage which caused the door to drop behind him.

Next morning the Field Director and his entourage had already loaded their luggage into a waiting car and were on the point of departure when a radio message arrived from the reconnaissance party to say that the tiger was in the trap. As can be imagined, excitement and elation swept through the camp, and everyone hastened to the scene of action.

The Field Director himself has given a vivid description of the scene: as they drew near the cage, he writes, an eerie hush prevailed over the area. No birds called, and even the ever-vociferous cicadas had fallen silent. Nothing could be seen of the heavily-camouflaged cage except the entrance, which by then was closed with a gate of steel bars.

Suddenly, at the approach of the domestic elephants with their human riders, there was an immense explosion of roars as the concealed tiger hurled himself towards his tormentors and the massive cage shook under its onslaught. The elephants trumpeted and panicked, and for a few moments pandemonium reigned. Once their mounts were back under control, the onlookers gathered round the cage, from which the tiger glared and snarled at his enemies.

Already his face and paws were a bloody mess of bruises and contusions, and in his struggle to free himself he had also smashed his nose. To save him from further injury it was decided to sedate him; but this was less simple than it seemed for his adrenal glands were in full production, and several extra doses of drugs were needed to knock him out. At last, by three p.m., he had been rendered unconscious.

The raging dynamo of a few minutes before now lay inert in the cage; but as the Field Director surveyed him, along with his research assistant and Brijendra Singh, a young volunteer conservationist and wildlife photographer who had come down from Delhi to help, the first qualms of conscience appear to have assailed them. Their flush of euphoria at having humbled the mighty carnivore quickly abated, to be replaced by the remorse which comes to anyone with human feelings who has destroyed a symbol.

Now that they had done it, they made hectic arrangements to convey the tiger to Lucknow Zoo as quickly as possible. Because of the difficulty of fording the flooded rivers, it was not until the next afternoon that the truck carrying the still-partially-sedated animal reached the zoo.

By then the tiger had spent forty hours in the trap, along with the remains of the rotting kill, which was full of maggots. His wounds had become infected, and he was induced to enter a squeeze cage so that his lacerated face and broken nose could be treated. Then for two days he touched neither food nor water. Yet soon he made an attempt to regain his freedom: at night, finding that the thick iron sheet which lined the floor of his prison was loose at one end, he prized it up with his paws and powerful jaws and tore it to shreds as though it were a piece of tinfoil.

Spattered with blood from his injured paws and belly, which had been ripped by the strips of torn-up iron, he was frantically working on the more vulnerable wooden planks underneath when the zoo staff discovered him making his bid for liberty. Had he escaped, it is anyone's guess what havoc he would have created before nemesis finally overtook him or he found temporary refuge in some outlying piece of forest, for there was no habitat suitable for a tiger anywhere near the zoo. As it was, he was immediately transferred to another cage, in which he seized a bar of angle iron and bent it double with his teeth, breaking one of his canines in the process. By now all his wounds were full of maggots.

In a somewhat premature report published in August 1981, 'A Complete Account of the First Successful Live Capture of a Free-Ranging, Man-Eating Tiger', the Field Director expressed the hope that 'Banga' would gradually become reconciled to the restrictions of his new existence. But it was not to be. Six months later the tiger made his final bid for freedom. His spirit broken by imprisonment and the battering he had received, he played his last card by dying, unobserved, in his cage. A post-mortem pronounced the cause of death as an infestation of tapeworms. This is a common ailment among wild tigers – perhaps because they sometimes eat putrescent flesh; but they normally recover quickly.

Whatever the immediate cause of the prisoner's demise, I am sure he would soon have died anyway, for it is my firm belief that a tiger which has lived wild and enjoyed the freedom of a large range cannot be expected to survive in captivity. There is no record of a tiger captured as an adult having lived for any length of time. To deny a wild creature its freedom is a crime against the laws of nature – and to believe anything else is futile self-deception.

The key question posed by the distressing incident was this: Should the tiger have been officially declared a man-eater in the first place? According to the criteria laid down by that great hunter-naturalist Jim Corbett, he should not. Corbett maintained that a tiger should be classed as a man-eater only if it had been shown that he sought human flesh compulsively (the Champawat and Panar man-eaters, for instance, killed 836 known humans). The Banga Jhala tiger never did this. He killed three men in twenty-eight months; the first died by accident, and the other two were on their own in the forest where no one had any business to go alone.

Whose fault was it that they died? The tiger had long since been declared India's national animal and strenuous efforts had been made to preserve it. Everyone concerned with the welfare of tigers had anticipated that, once the animals were fully protected, they would spill over out of the Corbett Park and colonise buffer areas of forest – exactly what had happened at Banga Jhala. There, this tiger's legitimate home had been encroached upon by illegal human habitation, and the wild-pig and deer on which he lived gunned down by crop-protection firearms. Humans had fallen into the habit of passing through the forest and lantana thickets in which he lived, never acknowledging that they were trespassers in tiger territory.

The fiasco of Banga Jhala precisely illustrates in microcosm the great problem which is the theme of this book. Can a Third-World democracy, with its population spiralling out of control towards the appalling figure of one billion people, afford living-space to the greatest predator on earth? Or will the huge effort of Project Tiger prove no more than a delaying action, a brief pause in the tiger's march towards extinction? As the twentieth century moves towards its end, we must ask – and try to answer – the question: *'Quo vadis, Panthera tigris?'*

2

DECLINE AND FALL

Modern animals evolved from the miacid, a small, insect-eating mammal whose direct descendants survive even today in the form of the viverrids, notably the genet of Africa. It is from the miacid that our modern cats are descended, via the *neofelids* and the *pseudaeluri*, which lived some twenty million years ago. One branch evolved into the sabre-tooth cats, which became extinct perhaps 10,000 years ago: contrary to popular supposition, the sabre-tooth was not an ancestor of our modern tiger, but rather a specialist which developed enormous fangs for stabbing large prey animals such as the mammoth and woolly rhinoceros.

It was an allied family which evolved into the cats of today. Originally grouped under the family name of *Felis*, they are now classified under two headings: the genus *Panthera*, or roaring cats, so-called because they have an elastic hyoid ligament in their larynx which enables them to produce a much greater volume of sound, and the genus *Felis*, or purring cats, which include all the smaller cats and the mountain lion, or cougar, of the New World. Throwback versions are the clouded leopard, the length of whose canines resembles that of the legendary sabre-tooth, and the cheetah. There is no doubt that the existence of all these species overlapped for a period, but eventually the ability of the conventional cats to subsist on a more catholic and variable diet enabled them to outlive the sabre-tooths, which followed their ponderous, slow-moving prey into oblivion.

From fossil remains found in the Arctic it is generally believed that tigers in their present form originated in Siberia. Over the millennia, as their population expanded, they spread southwards. Their invasion routes led through China, Indo-China and Burma to India, and southwards again through the Malay Peninsula to Sumatra, Java and Bali – where they arrived, presumably, before the islands separated from the mainland. (By an interesting contrast, they are not found either in Borneo or in Sri Lanka, even though the latter is so close to the Indian mainland.) Another route skirted the plateaux of Tibet, via the mountain passes of the Himalayas and the Pamirs. (Modern records show that tigers can live perfectly well at high altitudes: their existence has been recorded at 13,000 feet, and in 1899 a man-eater was reputed to have been shot at 10,000 feet near Mandali, in India.) From the Pamirs they moved westwards through Central Asia and Afghanistan to Northern Iran and the Caspian. Local advances were restricted by environmental and ecological conditions, but in the end they colonised almost the entire Asian Continent.

Eight sub-species have been identified. The nominate, or main, sub-species, is the Indian tiger, *Panthera tigris tigris*. The others are the Siberian (*P.t.Altaica*), the Chinese (*P.t. Amoyensis*), the Indo-Chinese (*P.t. Corbetti*), the Caspian (*P.t. Virgata*), the Sumatran (*P.t. Sumatrae*), the Javan (*P.t. Sondaica*) and the Balinese (*P.t. Balica*). Over the centuries each of these evolved into a slightly different form from the others, impelled by the rule of nature that warm-blooded mammals in cool climates tend to grow larger and have paler pigmentation than their counterparts in warmer climates with high humidity. Thus the Siberian tiger is the largest of all; it is distinguished by having a great deal of white on its face and chest, a thick tail, and a paler and thicker coat than other tigers, to enable it to survive in an arctic climate. Lengths of over thirteen feet have been recorded, and a maximum weight of 844 lbs.

Since all the eight sub-species spring from a common ancestor and yet are separately classified, it may well be asked why the human race, *homo sapiens*, though infinitely more prolific and diversified, has not been similarly classified. Why is it that we allow any human to breed with any other, and yet impose rigid controls on animals? The rigid scientific *diktat* against the interbreeding of animal sub-species has certainly accelerated the disappearance of some forms. Of the eight sub-species of tiger once extant, four are now either extinct or on the verge of becoming so, all through human antagonism. In China, for instance, men have always treated the tiger as an obstacle to human progress, and so have all-but eliminated it. In Bali, Java and the Caspian, humans have so ruined the tigers' habitat as to make their existence impossible. The only sub-species with a chance of survival are the Indian (with an estimated population of 3,000) the Indo-Chinese (2,000), the Sumatran (600–800) and the Siberian, whose residual population of 350–400 lives mainly in the Sikhote Alin reserve in Russia and two other reserves in Manchuria. Whether or not any of these survive in the long term depends entirely on the good will of human beings.

The Indian or Bengal tiger, with which this book is concerned, is smaller than the Siberian but larger than its southern neighbours. A stuffed specimen in the Smithsonian Museum in Washington, shot by a client of one of the shikar (or hunting) companies, is said to measure 11 ft 5 ½ ins from nose to tail-tip; and another, recorded by E. A. Smythies, a former Chief Conservator of Forests in Uttar Pradesh, weighed 705 lbs. These were both exceptional animals: the average length of a male Indian tiger is 9 ft 6 ins, and the average weight 400–450 lbs.

There is little doubt that for thousands of years, while vast areas of land were still covered by forests, tigers shared living space with man. It was only when humans began to fell timber on a large scale and clear wide areas for farming that the two species took up separate quarters. Rarely, if ever, can early man have killed a tiger, and thousands of years passed before humans conceived the idea of chasing the great predators for sport.

The earliest people known to have done this were the medieval Moghul emperors, who, being keen hunters, were also keen conservationists. The most bloodthirsty by far was Jehan-gir, who used to boast that in his active career he killed 14,000 animals and 17,000 birds. Paintings show him and his success-ors hunting tigers from elephant-back, but, as their weapons were restricted to bows and arrows, swords and spears, they probably did not kill any damaging number.

Their campaigns were slightly more effective against the lion, which had made its way into India from the north-west and lived in open habitats such as reed-beds, which were more easily negotiable than the hilly jungle favoured by tigers.

Sport-hunting was then an activity indulged in only by the rich and the courageous – and the odds on survival were not always with the hunter. An analogy can perhaps be traced with the pursuit of the lion by the Masai in East Africa: there the brave man who grabbed the surrounded lion by the tail was singled out from the rest of the El Morani, or soldier class, by the admiring women. Even so, it can safely be said that the hunting proclivities of the Moghul emperors posed no serious threat to the tigers' survival.

It was with the arrival of the East India Company in the seventeenth century that the picture started to change. With its colonial outlook and mandate for exploitation, the Company began to open up the forests as never before. Timber was needed for building, and later for railway sleepers; and when the administration of Great Britain's new possession passed from the private hands of Company servants to those of Government officials, more and more white men acquired a taste for pursuing the most powerful and dangerous of the great cats.

By the beginning of the nineteenth century tigers had reached the zenith of their territorial expansion in India: their population has been estimated at 40,000. They could be seen during the day on the roads just outside Calcutta, and Sir John Hewett, a former Governor of the United Provinces, recorded that the town of Gorakhpur, on the Indo-Nepalese border, had to be protected from their depredations by a line of fires kept alight all night. Small wonder that Victorian army officers and administrators saw the presence of so many dangerous carni-vores as a challenge which they could not resist.

It is worth examining the Victorians' attitude to tigers in

some detail, for it was largely they who gave the animal the bad name with which it is still burdened today. To them it was a ravening monster, the incarnation of evil, to be destroyed whenever possible. One writer after another portrayed it in the worst possible light, ascribing to it every conceivable vice, from cruelty, cowardice and general malignancy to taking a 'lustful pleasure' in killing. The tone was set by the formidable Captain H. Shakespear, whose book *The Wild Sports of India* was published in 1860. Completely ignoring the fact that tigers shun contact with mankind whenever possible, he assumed that they spent their lives poised to attack human targets. 'You will', he wrote, 'on no account whatever move in a jungle infested with tigers without your rifle in your hand and both barrels at full cock.' In the view of Shakespear and his contemporaries, the man who killed a tiger was a hero, and the tiger who killed a man (even in self-defence) a villain.

Many authors wrote in extravagant terms, but none more so than Major Walter Campbell, who published papers on Indian field sports in the *New Monthly Magazine* under the name 'The Old Forest Ranger' and later collected them into a book with that title. Like many fellow-officers, he saw the operation of big-game hunting in military terms: the tiger was invariably 'the enemy', the jungle 'the battlefield', each expedition 'a campaign', and the death of a tiger a 'glorious victory'.

One sentence, describing a tiger entangled in a net, epitomises Campbell's style and attitude: 'A hellish fire shot from his eyes, and his whiskered lips curled into a grin of ineffable malignity as he gathered himself together for a decisive spring.' Every encounter is described in the exaggerated, melodramatic style of a cheap novel. Here a wounded tiger is seen creeping towards the shikar party through the long grass:

'Now for it, lads! Death or victory!' said Mansfield in a low, firm tone of voice, his proud lip curling haughtily as he drew himself up to his full height and half raised the rifle to his shoulder. 'Be steady – don't throw your shots away; there is life or death in every ounce of lead. Ha! – '

At this critical moment he caught a hasty glimpse of the tiger's malignant green eyes as he lowered his head for the fatal spring. Like a flash of lightning the trusty rifle poured forth its deadly contents. A roar

— a bound — and the stricken monster rolled gasping at their feet, with a two-ounce ball buried in his skull.

Other authors blackened the animal's character with equal assiduity. 'In reality the tiger is not the audacious, foolhardy animal the generality of tiger stories portray,' wrote the Hon. James Inglis in *Tent Life in Tigerland*. 'He is more commonly a cunning, sneaking rogue . . . the cruel, whiskered robber . . . You know not but that some hungry beast is gloating greedily with looks of fear upon his natural enemy — man . . . What an embodiment of devilish cruelty, of hate and savagery incarnate!'

Almost everyone took it for granted that the only thing to do with a tiger was to kill it. Yet it was typical of the Victorians that they should also demand that the killing be done in sporting manner. The sentiment was perfectly expressed by J. Moray Brown in his book *Shikar Sketches*:

He died as a tiger *ought* to die — tracked, met face to face, and fought on his own ground by four *sportsmen*, and not done to death by that low, villainous system of poisoning.

The degrees of sportsmanship exhibited by the hunters varied enormously. Some men were brave enough — or fool-hardy enough — to try to stalk tigers on foot, but most preferred either to hire elephants and operate from the security of howdahs on their backs, or else to engage a small army of beaters and sit up trees waiting for the quarry to be driven past. Few, in any case, had ideas as debased as those of the Indian Rajah who sought to curry favour with an officer known as 'Felix' by bringing him a very fine panther (or leopard) in a cage and suggesting that he might be amused to shoot it through the bars.

'Felix' declined the offer, but his subsequent conduct scarcely does him more credit than if he had accepted it. To give himself a sporting shot, he rigged up a pulley and opened the trap door of its cage from a distance. As the animal bolted he took a shot at it with a double-barrelled rifle, but only wounded it, whereupon it leapt on to one of the Sepoys who had come to watch:

The beast was fixed claws and jaws on the man, and I felt very uncomfortable, as no doubt also did the Sepoy. There was only one course open to me consistent with safety, namely to put the barrel of the rifle against the panther and blow him away. This I did ... The Sepoy recovered after six months in hospital. My C.O. gave me a wigging for this, and suggested that I had endangered the lives of the community in cantonments; but I replied that wild beasts when hunted did not, as a rule, walk into bungalows, but preferred rural retreats, in which reply I was considered flippant.

It seems just as well that 'Felix' sheltered behind a pseudonym, for in his arrogance, his facetiousness and his bloodthirsty outlook, he was surely the quintessential Victorian.

That nineteenth-century India was a wonderful place for the rifleman, there can be no doubt. Describing his operations during the 1850s in the thickly-wooded ravines which held the tigers, Major General William Rice recalled: 'Never was there such a paradise for the hunter ... the whole country then being like an undiscovered land, for on the best district maps was written for miles around, "No information forthcoming on this part".' No wonder Rice describes tiger-shooting as 'the most exciting and glorious sport this world affords'.

The multiple accounts make it all too clear that if anyone took a lustful pleasure in killing, it was the British officers and administrators. C. E. Gouldsbury, late of the Indian Police, spoke for hundreds of them when he wrote:

A tiger, seen for the first time at large in its own jungles, is a sight few sportsmen can look on without experiencing a feeling of intense excitement, coupled with an almost uncontrollable desire to possess its head and skin.

Yet among the bloodthirsty chorus, one or two wiser voices were raised. G. P. Sanderson, the officer in charge of the Government elephant-catching station at Mysore, was himself a keen tiger-shooter, but at least he had the sense to appreciate the predator's role in the natural scheme of things. It was not the tiger which ruined villagers' crops, he pointed out, but rather the deer and pig whose numbers the tiger kept down.

Were the tiger and the panther gone, they [the crop-eaters] would soon gain the upper hand . . . Cultivation would recede in many parts of the country . . . The tiger is no unmitigated evil in the land. His pursuit affords excitement and recreation to many a hard-worked official whose life, except for an occasional day in the jungles, would be one of uninterrupted toil . . . It is a pity to see the tiger proscribed and hunted to death by every unsportsmanlike method that can be devised, in response to popular outcries – chiefly in England – without foundation in fact, about his destructiveness. Trace out and slay every man-eater by all means possible, and at any expense; but ordinary tigers are exceedingly inoffensive, and have their uses. May the day be far distant when the tiger shall become practically extinct!

Sanderson sounded that note of prophetic warning in 1878, and by then many of the hunters were complaining that tigers had become far scarcer than half a century before. Yet two factors, apart from their own blood-lust, incited them to keep on with the slaughter. One was the fact that tigers were officially vermin, and that the government paid a bounty for every one killed; the other, the enormous gratitude which the death of every tiger evoked among inhabitants of the area in which it was killed. Even if the beast was not a man-eater, villagers were always delighted to be rid of a predator which had been eating their cattle. The local people 'got drunk over the victory', wrote 'Felix', who during his twenty-six years in India shot thirty-one tigers, eighteen leopards and twenty-five bears: 'After the death of the tiger I was master of the village. Every man in it was at my service . . . '

Sometimes, of course, a tiger managed to retaliate effectively. Lieutenant Colonel W. Gordon Cumming described how a friend of his called Bulkley was seized by a wounded tiger which sunk its teeth in his back and carried him for twenty yards before dropping him. Bulkley was lucky: having had his wounds washed and poulticed with flour, he was borne eighty miles on a bed to the cantonment at Baroda, and eventually recovered, after an operation on his shoulder.

Another friend, Langton, was less fortunate. Bitten through the elbow and thumb, he had to endure a three-day journey back to Baroda. There he was put to bed, but 'he soon fell into a drowzy state, from which he never recovered . . . All that was possible was done for Langton, but he never rallied, and died in the afternoon.' His demise was ascribed to shock exacerbated by exposure to the sun. On another expedition Gordon Cumming's native gun-bearer, Foorsut, was dragged down out of a tree by a tiger and bitten through the thigh. On the first day after the accident he seemed fairly well, but on the second his companions noticed 'a slight twitching of the points of the fingers', and by four p.m. he was dead.

Such successes on the part of the hunted were all too few. The number of tigers continued to fall, and their decline was brutally accelerated during the 1880s by the advent of Express rifles, much more powerful than the smooth-bore or primitively-rifled weapons which had been in vogue until then. 'For many years the diminution of Indian game has been a subject for remark,' wrote Captain A. I. R. Glasfurd in 1902, 'and the greater proportion of the country is still being rapidly depleted . . .' Glasfurd, like others, laid only part of the blame on the white hunters. Abundant evidence showed, he said, that 'the real root of the evil lies in the depredations of the native shikaris – trappers, snarers, shooters, but especially the shooters . . . The marked diminution of game dates from the time when serviceable guns became cheap and easy of purchase by native shikaris.'

To prove his point, he quoted the returns of Government awards for wild animals killed from one typical district. In one period under review, licensed sportsmen shot fourteen tigers, nine leopards and eleven bears, and the natives thirty-one, fifty-two and forty-two respectively. Besides, 'for each one of such dangerous animals slain, a very large number of deer and other harmless creatures must be made away with.' In the course of his researches Glasfurd found one taxidermist who paid fifty rupees for a tiger skin and sold it for 300 when he had cured it.

The arrival of cordite powder, at the turn of the century, made weapons still more efficient; but the tigers gained a temporary respite during the First World War. Just as during the Mutiny in 1857, when, in Glasfurd's words, 'the native gun retired into a remarkably strict condition of purdah,' and game of all kinds increased to an extraordinary extent, so during the Great War the aggression of potential hunters was distracted elsewhere. According to A. A. Dunbar Brander, writing in 1923, 'The war practically put an end to shooting, except by District Officers, and during its duration the tigers rapidly increased.'

One result of the build-up, he reported, seemed to be 'a very large increase in the number of man-eaters. Hardly a gazette is issued without announcing special awards for about twenty different animals . . . It is possible that the rapid increase in the number of tigers during the war, with no increase in the food supply, but rather the reverse, has led to the present conditions.'

Dunbar Brander was a curious character. A zoologist by education, he worked as a forester in the Central Provinces – now Madhya Pradesh – and was known among his subordinates as 'Danda Mar Bandar', or 'Hit the Monkey with a Stick', a vernacular rendering of his name which suited him admirably, as he was a peppery fellow, given to driving his car round and round the forest resthouse in which he lived so that he could claim his full travel allowance from the mileage.

No mean naturalist, Dunbar Brander has been honoured by having the hard-ground species of barasingha named after him. He was much interested in tigers, and studied them carefully. For six years he more or less gave up shooting, and had the grace to admit that 'one can see so much more of an animal, and under such different circumstances, if one is not intent on killing it.' Clearly he admired tigers, and wrote lyrically of their physical grace:

While questing through the jungle the tiger glides silently along. He seems to flow past one like a phantom. This impression is created by his silent tread, but more so by his action, which seems specially adapted for concealment. Both limbs on the same side move together, or almost so, and it is this which produces the gliding effect.

Had Dunbar Brander lived and written half a century later, he might, I feel, have taken a prominent part in the campaign to save the tiger, for he was at heart a conservationist. Yet in the 1920s, when his book, *Wild Animals in Central India*, was published, there were still enough tigers about, and attitudes against them were still hard enough, for him to write:

'A cat has nine lives', and the tiger is the largest, strongest cat in the world . . . It is a golden rule to look upon any [wounded] tiger which shows the slightest signs of life as a highly dangerous animal, and lead should be poured into it until all signs of animation have ceased.

The first man who felt real sympathy for tigers – the first man who championed their cause – was already at work in the jungles round his home in Naini Tal. But Jim Corbett was no self-seeking publicist, and the world had to wait another twenty years before he was persuaded to publish his marvellous stories.

If the attitude of the Victorian and Edwardian British towards tigers now seems monstrous, that of leading Indians was little better. Under the ruling princes – a bulwark of the Raj – hunting degenerated into a form of patronage. The finest form of entertaining which the princes could devise was an elaborate tiger hunt, to which they would invite the Governor or even the Viceroy in the hope of securing favours.

The princely hunts were held on an enormous scale, as were those staged by the Maharajah of Nepal, with huge numbers of elephants specially assembled for the task. The method most often employed was that of a ring: the beating elephants – as many as 400 or 500 – enclosed a large area of ground within a complete circle, and the riflemen, mounted on other elephants, rode into the centre of the ring to shoot the tigers trapped there. By such methods, in 1911, King George V and his party despatched thirty-nine tigers in eleven days, and in a prolonged operation during 1919 and 1920 no fewer than 120 tigers were killed in three months.

No doubt the proceedings had a certain tinsel glamour and excitement. As the combatants surged about in the sea of 25-foot grass, with the sal forest looming dark in the background, the roars of the tigers dominated the trumpeting of the frightened elephants and the raucous yells of encouragement from their handlers, lending the scene a touch of primordial wildness as the mighty predator battled for existence. In fact the tigers never had a chance against the vastly superior human forces, with their deadly modern rifles. In the evenings, when the pandemonium subsided and the sundowners toasted yet another day's slaughter, the silence that settled was the silence of the grave.

Still more damaging than these occasional large-scale manoeuvres were the personal ambitions of some maharajahs, who shot vast numbers of tigers as a means of boosting their own status. The most notorious was the Maharajah of Sarguja, in Central India, who, in the early part of this century, is supposed to have accounted for 1,157 tigers even though, possessing only one serviceable eye, he had to use a contortionist's grip and fire off his left shoulder. So keen was he to achieve an unsurpassable score that he is said to have included unborn foetuses in his total. Another mass-murderer was the old Maharajah of Rewa, who paced Sarguja to a score of 500. His son and heir then opted out of the race to become famous as the owner of Mohan, first of the celebrated line of the Rewa white tigers. Old Man Sarguja, however, continued his nefarious activities until called to account, having exceeded the proverbial three-score years and ten.

Even with so many people after their blood, tigers remained relatively numerous during the 1920s, and it was then that I myself first became aware of them. For ten years, from 1923 to 1932, I lived in the State of Balrampur, where my father was the Chief Executive, appointed to manage the affairs of the Maharajah, who was a minor. Balrampur was part of the administrative district of Gonda, which ran right to the Nepal hills, and its Zemindary forests – so called from the feudal system of tenure which still existed at that date – were renowned for the wealth of big game which they harboured. This abundance was due largely to the fact that the forests grew on the Bhabar – the gravelly belt of land lying immediately below the hills, where the soil had been formed from the detritus of pebbles and smashed boulders washed down by the annual floods. In contrast with the lush, low-lying Terai, which borders it, the Bhabar has shallow soil and a low water-table, and grows timber of inferior quality; but it is still ideal for wildlife.

Growing up as a boy in a household which regarded big-game shooting as a normal part of life, I took to it with an enthusiasm of which I now feel thoroughly ashamed. I shot my first leopard at the age of twelve, and my first tiger at fourteen: in those days of relative plenty there seemed nothing morally wrong in driving tigers out of the long grass with elephants or sitting up trees to ambush them.

One reason, no doubt, was the apparently inexhaustible supply of tigers. Although the population never seemed to expand, every favourite niche of habitat remained full: as soon as one tiger was shot, another would move in to take its place. We came to realise not only that a reservoir of tigers existed in the vast virgin forests of Nepal – particularly in the mountain and sub-montane jungles of the Churia range – but also that some means of communication between far-flung tigers ensured that a range never remained unoccupied for long. Similar conditions seemed to exist all along the 1,000-mile border between the two countries: what India shot, Nepal replaced. Over the past century, however, the tigers had learned their lesson. They did their best to avoid the proximity of man, and in fact there seemed to be an inviolable line which they did not cross: they were never found in the forest next to populated districts, even though the area contained an abundance of prey animals and was frequented by leopards – the mere presence of humans kept them back.

By then, in India, elaborate rules for conservation had been established, and strict limits were imposed on the bags shot. On the other side of the border a different system prevailed. In Nepal only the King and the ruling Rana families were allowed to hunt, and such were the difficulties of transport and communication in the mountain kingdom that it was the exception rather than the rule for a tiger-hunt to be held in the same area every year. The tigers in both countries thus lived moderately sheltered lives, shaped on the one hand by their own ability to coexist among themselves, and on the other by their ingrained abhorrence of the human race, which made them give men as wide a berth as possible. So wary were they in Balrampur that, as children with a penchant for firing at anything which moved, we had strict instructions that on any serious tiger-hunt there was to be no shooting for the pot within at least two miles of tiger covert – a prohibition which seemed pretty pointless to

Right *The man-eater of Banga Jhala*

us, but which showed the importance attached by our mentors to their highest form of sport.

During the Second World War the tigers of India again won a temporary respite while the human race slaughtered its own kind in fratricidal conflict. Yet at the same time the destruction of wildlife habitat accelerated to a pace never seen before, as the forests were recklessly plundered for timber.

Then, soon after peace had been re-established, came Independence, and – for tigers – the beginning of the end. Quickly the feeling spread abroad that all men are equal (even if some are more equal than others), but that animals, having no vote, have no right to exist. The exemplary organisation of forests established by the British began to collapse. The carefully-worked-out rules for conservation were abandoned. Modern technology, in the form of the chain-saw, the bull-dozer, the ubiquitous Jeep, the searchlight and the automatic weapon, hastened the destruction of habitat and wildlife alike. Worst of all, a furiously-expanding human population began to invade and erode the jungles in search of living space: millions of acres which had once belonged to the animals were wrested away by humans desperately needing land on which to grow food.

The tiger, though hard-pressed, was still blackguarded and reviled. Although a supremely adaptable animal, he had by then come almost to the end of the great journey which his ancestors began in the Chigar Caves of Siberia several million years before. There is no doubt that in antiquity, while he was actively colonising his advance under pressure of his own expanding population, he was an aggressor: it cannot be expected that a predator of his dimensions would be anything else. But since the beginning of the nineteenth century he had been on the defensive, and had done everything he could to avoid clashes with man. His only reward for self-effacement had been persecution; now, when the humans have at last relented and tried to rescue him, it is almost too late.

Above *'The Man-eater's Victim': a Victorian view*
Below *Early-nineteenth-century hunting camp*

3

A LARGE-HEARTED GENTLEMAN

Man-Eaters of Kumaon, first published in 1944, is easily the most famous book about tigers ever written. The stories of how Jim Corbett stalked and shot man-eating tigers in the jungles of the Kumaon hills have gripped readers all over the world, partly because of the author's great natural gift of narrative, and partly because his qualities as an exceptionally civilised human being shine through the text.

Corbett was far ahead of his contemporaries, both in his attitude towards wild animals and in his ideas about conservation. It can truly be said that although he shot tigers when he had to, he was the first man who really cared about their welfare.

His father, Christopher William Corbett, came out to India as a civil engineer in Government service and did so well for himself that he acquired a considerable amount of property in the hill station of Naini Tal, as well as a forest estate called Choti Haldwani and a winter residence at Kaladhungi. Jim himself had a modest job with the railways, at Mokameh Ghat, supervising the trans-shipment of goods from one railway system to another. It was his hobby, rather than his work, that made him famous: though always busy in his office, he never failed to respond to the appeals of the hill-folk who had been terrorised by man-eaters.

His destruction of the Champawat man-eating tigress in 1907, the man-eating leopard of Panar in 1910, and the Muktesar tigress in 1911 laid the foundations of a legend that grew throughout his lifetime and continued to blossom after his death. By the time the First World War broke out he had built up such a reputation for honesty and hard work that he was able to recruit a volunteer labour force which he took to Meso-potamia; at the same time, the loyalty which he commanded among his railway staff inspired them to carry on their trans-shipment work with the same efficiency while he was away. After the war the hunting of man-eaters became his main activity: his epic pursuit of the leopard of Rudraprayag lasted from 1918 until 1926, and that of the Chowgarh tigers from 1926 to 1930. He continued his arduous expeditions far past the age at which most men would have stopped, and when he shot the Thak man-eater in 1938 he was already 63.

To every boy who grew up during the 1920s in an Indian home with an interest in wildlife, Corbett was something of a hero; but to me he was a figure of special reverence, for I was lucky enough to know him well. This came about because my father had chosen Naini Tal, 6,300 feet up in the Himalayan foothills, as a place of retreat for the family in the hot weather and the monsoon, and during one of his spells of leave there he happened to meet Corbett.

The hill station – spectacularly sited with a background of distant snow peaks – was the summer capital for the British administration of the United Provinces; the Governor would arrive by the end of April, and remain in residence until the end of September. Local administrators would come up for various periods of recessional during the monsoon months from mid-June to mid-September, but little work was done, and the atmosphere was one of relaxation from bearing the White Man's Burden.

Naini Tal was – and is – a lovely place, with steep hills girdling a lake two miles long and one mile wide in the shape of a tear-drop. Geologists differ as to the lake's origin. Some attribute it to glaciers and landslides, others to volcanic action.

Legend, however, has it that three sages, arriving on a penitential pilgrimage at the crest of the hill called Cheena, and finding no water, dug a hole at the foot of the mountain and siphoned water into it from a holy lake of Mansarowar in Tibet. After the sages had departed, the goddess Naini arrived to take up residence in the waters of the lake which now bears her name.

Rumours of the holy lake's existence reached British administrators early in the nineteenth century, but the local inhabitants were unwilling to disclose its situation – until in 1839 one of the British hit on the ingenious plan of placing a large stone on the head of a hillman and telling him he would have to carry it until he arrived at the Goddess's abode. After many days of diversionary wandering (it is said) the man was so exhausted that he finally led the party to the lake.

A century later the stone was still being exhibited to interested inquirers, among them Jim Corbett. It looked to him as though the lump of rock must weigh about 600 lbs, but when he expressed doubt a hillman replied that in those days people used to be very strong. The story may be apocryphal, but certainly more recent records have it that a woman carried a grand piano up the hill to Naini Tal.

At the head of the lake are the playing fields known as the Flats, and the temple of Naina Devi, where Corbett buried the human fingers found in the stomach of the Champawat man-eater. A gravel road encircling the water leads to a sheer cliff known as Smugglers' Rock. In those days it was presided over by an old Brahmin priest, whom Corbett knew well, and from the vantage-point of the rock – now a favourite take-off site for unrequited lovers and failed examinees – one could look down into the clear water and see large schools of mahseer, the famous fighting fish of India, which might weigh over 100 lbs. Now, alas, the waters are opaque with pollution and devoid of life, although departed spirits are still said to haunt the precincts at night.

In the days of the Raj, Government House was perched on the summit of the hill known as Ayarpata, and residential houses clung to the surrounding hill slopes, with Philander Smith College, the school at which Jim had been educated, opposite on the mountain called Sher Ka Danda (Path of the Tiger), sitting on a knife-edge ridge that overlooked the rolling hills to the north. The mainstream of life flowed round the lower slopes above the lake; a little way above the shops, hotels and places of entertainment stood the Amateur Dramatic Society's Club, known as the Chalet, where dances were held and local talent put on Gilbert & Sullivan operettas. Finally, on the edge of the lake itself was the Naini Tal Boat Club, an exclusive, white man's social precinct where the main recreation was sailing. The story was told of how Robert Anderson, head of a gentlemen's outfitters' firm and mainstay of the acting fraternity, applied for membership of the Boat Club, only to be blackballed by the President, Sir William Stampe, with the remark: 'If I wish to see my tailor, I shall go to his shop!'

Such was the ultra-British nature of Jim Corbett's home town. Our own family's home was Jubilee Hall, the highest house on the hill topped by the Cheena Peak, and within walking distance of the Corbett establishment, Gurney House.

I was first introduced to Jim soon after he had killed the man-eating leopard of Rudraprayag, which had terrorised the pilgrims on the route to Badrinath for eight long years. At once I was fascinated by the tales of his adventures, and by his stories of the occult – such as the one about lights which appeared at certain seasons on the steep hillside of Purnagiri, above the Sarda Gorge, and for which there was no explanation. At last I plucked up enough courage to ask if I might come and see him, and I was thrilled when he suggested that I should pay him a visit every Sunday, early in the morning.

Little did he realise what he was letting himself in for! Now that I know how tiresome it is to be pestered with questions by children, however well-meaning, I marvel at the patience with which he endured my weekly inquisition. As for me – each visit was an experience in itself. In my memory, almost every Sunday morning was wet. The night before I used to lie in bed, listening to the rain drumming on the roof, and pray for a clear morning, but always dawn seemed to break dark and murky: the clouds gave no sign of lifting as I donned my little mackintosh, opened my umbrella and stepped out into the pouring rain on my three-mile walk. The low-flying vapours seemed to race past me as I hurried downhill to the Flats and began the climb to Gurney House on the upper slopes of Ayarpata. A light would be burning in Jim's study, for the gloom was all-pervading, and as I entered the warm room his brown-and-white spaniel, Robin, would get up to investigate the newcomer.

The next hour was pure magic. And yet, entranced as I was, I did not realise how privileged I had become, for the stories I heard were not published for another twenty years. What I do remember is the breathless thrill I felt every time a tale moved towards its climax. As I heard about the Temple Tiger, and the Himalayan bear who had the courage and ability to drive him off his kill, I felt desperately sorry that the bear should be gunned down in his hour of victory. I could almost feel, in my own small hand, the two nightjar eggs, cradled in moss, which had saved Jim from one of the Chowgarh man-eaters: when he suddenly saw that the tigress was only eight feet from him, the fact that he held the eggs in his left hand prevented him making any sudden movement. Using his right hand only, he brought the rifle round as smoothly as he could, and his enforced slow-motion forestalled the tigress's charge. I was particularly glad to know that once the tigress was dead he returned the two eggs (which he had taken for his collection) to their 'little depression in the rock that did duty as a nest', and later saw that the hen nightjar had returned to brood them. He was, as he said, highly superstitious, and believed that the eggs had brought him luck.

No less thrilling was the climax of his hunt for the Mohan man-eater. Creeping forward with all possible stealth, he spotted a black-and-yellow object some three inches long, which after some scrutiny he realised was the tip of the tiger's tail. At first he thought the animal was poised to spring on him:

The tip of the tail was twenty feet from me, and allowing eight feet for the tiger's length while crouching, his head would be twelve feet away. But I should have to approach much nearer before I should be able to see enough of his body to get in a crippling shot . . .

Inch by inch I again started to creep forward until the whole of the tail, and after it the hindquarters, came into view. When I saw the hindquarters I could have shouted with delight, for they showed that the tiger was not crouching and ready to spring, but was lying down . . .

Another foot forward and his belly came into view, and from the regular way in which it was heaving up and down I knew that he was asleep.

The fact that he shot the Mohan man-eater in his sleep troubled Jim deeply, for the act seemed somehow unsporting; and when eventually he described the event in *Man-Eaters of Kumaon*, he analysed his feelings with typical honesty:

The finish had not been satisfactory, for I had killed the animal, that was lying five feet from me, in his sleep . . . The arguments [for shooting him thus] were
   a. the tiger was a man-eater that was better dead than alive;
   b. therefore it made no difference whether he was awake or asleep when killed, and
   c. that had I walked away when I saw his belly heaving up and down I should have been morally responsible for the deaths of all human beings he killed thereafter.
All good and sound arguments, you will admit, for my having acted as I did; but the regret remains that through fear of the consequences to myself, or fear of losing the only chance I might ever get, or possibly a combination of the two, I did not awaken the sleeping animal and give him a sporting chance.

Such moral scruples were rather above my boyish head, but the excitement of hearing the story has never faded.

Later in the morning Jim's half-sister Mary Doyle would appear. A handsome, white-haired lady, considerably older than he, she used to bake the most marvellous seed-cake, which I greedily devoured. His wife, Maggie, would also come in, but she was rather withdrawn, and my young memory recalls only a background presence.

Sometimes my father would go out walking with Jim, and he would return with accounts of hair-raising climbs, for his guide was as sure-footed as a mountain goat, and appeared unaffected by heights. One day he took my father and me up the rock face of Deopata, next to the Cheena Peak, and we had to creep across a slab of solid rock above a drop which seemed to plunge all the way to Kaladhungi. I was almost paralysed by fright, and I remember afterwards my mother was furious with my father for having exposed me to such a risk. On another occasion our route led to the top of a pine tree, which one then had to sway, so as to be flung on to the top of a cliff, but I was not allowed to attempt the jump. Soon after this Jim suddenly arrived at our house proposing to take me with him to hunt the biggest leopard in the Kumaon hills. Alas, I was not at home, and at the time counted this the greatest disappointment of my life.

Having had a rather sickly boyhood, I had always been tutored at home. But in 1932, when I was twelve, my father was transferred away from Balrampur, and decided that I should go to a boarding school, albeit as a day-scholar. As I had by then discovered that Jim had been educated at Philander Smith's College, in Naini Tal, and also that Busher, the Principal, had been a class-mate of his, I persuaded my father to send me there. Thus I entered the Junior Cambridge Class, and stayed with the Headmaster, F. G. Brandon, known as 'Barney'.

It was unfortunate that I did not go as an ordinary boarder, and, in the manner of schools the world over, the boys were doubly unkind when they found I was living with authority. Yet there were ample compensations. From the classroom I could watch the great lammergeiers quartering the skies above the mountain crags, and surrounding the house in which I lived was dense oak forest, where I imagined man-eaters might be lurking. I built myself a hut of branches and leaves, in which I used to study, and one evening, hearing a slight sound, I looked up into the double barrels of Old Man Busher's gun, as he was out looking for pine martens.

After a bit, school became fun, and I recounted – much to the amusement of the other boys, especially the ones who had borne the weight of a caning from the headmaster's dextrous wrist – how the stern old Barney used to practise the yo-yo every evening. One morning, as we all looked out of the classroom window, we saw to our astonishment the kindergarten class crawling up the hill-slope eating grass, having been ordered to do so by Miss Mooney, their teacher, as a punishment for some minor misdemeanour.

Once I had left school and Naini Tal I lost contact with Jim for a while. While I completed a formal and undistinguished education, he put an end to the Kanda man-eater in 1933, the Chuka man-eater in 1936 and the Thak man-eater in 1938.

During the Second World War, while I joined the Army and did a stint of overseas service, he was specially asked by the military authorities to organise a jungle warfare training camp in what is now the state of Madhya Pradesh, with the honorary rank of lieutenant colonel. His great subject was living in – and off – the jungle, and those who were taught by him never forgot it. By then he was close to 70, and the strain of the war broke his health: a severe illness, brought on by the rigorous conditions of the training camp, was exacerbated by his own characteristic refusal to spare himself hardships.

In 1946 the British Government conferred upon him the Companionship of the Indian Empire – a distinction usually bestowed on senior bureaucrats for meritorious administrative service. Then, as Independence approached in 1947, he decided with a heavy heart that he must leave the country in which he had spent all his life. When I met him again not long before his departure, he told me that he was heartbroken to be leaving; but, like many of their friends, his wife, Maggie, felt that their lives might be endangered in the turmoil which they thought was bound to greet the hand-over of power to the people of India.

To anyone who knew of Jim's standing in the local community, it was obvious that such fears were utterly unfounded: no harm could possibly have come to him if he had stayed. Yet the political metamorphosis seemed so enormous at the time that it defied rational consideration, and the Corbetts emigrated to a coffee plantation in Kenya, which Jim owned jointly with two other retired British civil servants. His last words to me before he left were that he would like me to take over the plantation before he died, since he was the youngest of the three partners, and none of them had any children. This pipe-dream, like many others, never came to fruition.

In 1952 he received a small honour which very much pleased him, being asked to join the party of Princess Elizabeth and her husband Prince Philip when they visited Tree Tops, the famous hotel built on stilts in the Aberdare Mountains. On the historic night during which her father King George VI died, and the Princess became Queen, Jim spent the hours of darkness sitting with a loaded rifle at the top of the ladder which reached down among the hotel's legs to the ground. The royal party believed that his job was to protect them against wild animals, but in fact he was there for a more sinister reason. Mau Mau terrorists had already begun to threaten the Whites of Kenya, and Mervyn Cowie, Director of Kenya's National Parks, had got hold of Jim, as the man he trusted most in the world, to make sure that no incident occurred. In a small book which he wrote describing the assignation, Jim typically did not reveal his true role; but he did leave a memorable description of how once, during the night, he felt the ladder move as some creature brushed against it down below.

So modest was he that he might never have published anything at all, had it not been for special pleading by his friends. During my boyhood I had often, at my father's suggestion, besought him to write down the marvellous stories that he told me; but he always brushed the idea aside on the grounds that not enough people would be interested. Only when he saw an opportunity of benefiting someone else did he finally allow the tales to be printed: when *Man-Eaters of Kumaon* came out in 1944, the royalties from the first edition went to a charity for Indian soldiers blinded during the war.

Indians love to deify the departed, and Jim, already a legend in his lifetime, has now almost achieved apotheosis. Although it is over thirty-five years since he left Naini Tal, having bequeathed his property to his retainers, his name lives on as vigorously as ever, not least in the Corbett National Park, which now embraces some of his old hunting grounds. Another distinction, posthumously conferred, was the re-naming of the Indo-Chinese tiger, which is now called *Panthera tigris corbetti*, after him.

His achievement as a conservationist is impossible to measure in finite terms. He founded India's first conservation magazine, before the Second World War, but after his departure it lost impetus, for there was no one to be the standard-bearer; and it cannot be said that he achieved a great deal in practical terms. Yet his importance lay in what he thought and wrote rather than in what he did.

Today, in the 1980s, the idea of conserving wildlife has become an integral part of civilised thought, and the assumption that human beings may interfere with the normal processes of evolution, on the principle of might prevailing over right, is now seen as a barbaric concept. Fifty or sixty years ago, when Corbett was in his heyday, things were very different. In those days sport-hunting was all the vogue, and everyone shot everything as a matter of course. To advocate restraint was considered eccentric, and when Corbett emerged as a champion of the big cats, many people thought him a crank.

His views, however, were definite and clearly-stated. In the preface to *Man-Eaters of Kumaon* he wrote:

The author who first used the words 'as cruel as a tiger' and 'as bloodthirsty as a tiger', when attempting to emphasise the evil character of the villain of his piece, not only showed a lamentable ignorance of the animal he defamed, but coined phrases which have come into universal circulation and which are mainly responsible for the wrong opinion of tigers held by all except that very small proportion of the public who have the opportunity of forming their own opinions.

After giving a charming sketch of himself as a small boy, wandering day and night through the jungle armed with an old, muzzle-loading gun lashed together with brass wire, sleeping by the fire, and frequently meeting tigers at close quarters, he went on to say that he had never known an instance where a tiger had been bloodthirsty, or had killed without provocation more than it needed to feed itself and its cubs:

A tiger's function in the scheme of things is to help maintain the balance in nature and if, on rare occasions when driven by dire necessity he kills a human being, or, when his natural food has been ruthlessly exterminated by man, he kills two per cent of the cattle he is alleged to have killed, it is not fair that for these acts a whole species should be branded as being cruel and bloodthirsty . . .

The tiger is a large-hearted gentleman with boundless courage, and . . . when he is exterminated — as exterminated he will be unless public opinion rallies to his support — India will be the poorer by having lost the finest of her fauna.

It is instructive to compare Corbett with two of his contemporaries who also published books about Indian wildlife. Both were professional foresters, who came into contact with animals simply because the creatures lived in the forests they looked after. One – A. A. Dunbar Brander – we have already met; as I have said, he showed a genuine interest in animals and became knowledgeable about them, but still advocated pumping wounded tigers full of lead. The other was F. W. Champion, formerly a forest officer in what was then the United Provinces, who published two very readable books – *With a Camera in Tigerland* and *The Jungle in Sunlight and Shadow* – both full of outstanding wildlife photographs. To him photography was an engrossing hobby, a more civilised version of the bloodsports indulged in by his colleagues: he would set up his camera in the evening, and collect the results next morning, after a night's rest, before taking up his normal forestry duties during the day. His books are full of interest, but nowhere in them does he express concern for the future of the animals and their habitat.

Where Dunbar Brander observed and shot, where Champion observed and recorded, Corbett pondered, felt for the animals, and worried about what would happen to them in the long term. He was one of those men who, by living close to nature, acquire an empathy with wild creatures which makes them regard their trials and tribulations, their joys and sorrows, much as they regard those of their own kind. Lord Hailey, a former Governor of the United Provinces, who knew him well, wrote of him:

I do not know how far the picture formed of him by his readers differs from that which will live in the memory of his friends. In one respect perhaps the reader who has known him through his books may have some advantage over him. He seldom spoke of the hardships and dangers of those encounters with man-eaters which gave such an incomparable thrill to his record of them. He felt, I think, that these were matters which lay between him and the great beasts whose strength and courage he respected, and whose lapses into ways that were a menace to man he could in due season forget.

Plenty of attempts have been made to denigrate Corbett, and to show that he shot for sport as readily as his contemporaries – witness his killing of the Bachelor of Powalgarh, which was not a man-eater, but had merely gained notoriety by eluding hunters for ten years. Similarly, the Pipal Pani tiger was not a man-eater, but Corbett shot it on the grounds that it might become dangerous after a villager had wounded it with his muzzle-loader.

In these instances he does seem to have hunted for sport. But the fact that he did sometimes indulge in the normal practice of his time need not detract from his main achievement: in devoting immense amounts of time and energy to the pursuit of man-eaters, his aim was to free local communities from the reigns of terror which the predators had established.

It is easy to forget the scale on which the man-eaters operated. The Champawat and Panar tigers between them killed a recorded total of 836 humans, and probably many more that went unaccounted. The Chowgarh tiger and the Rudraprayag leopard were active for four and eight years respectively. Time and again Corbett would find a community paralysed by fear:

The people of the village, numbering some fifty men, women and children, were in a state of abject terror, and though the sun was well up when I arrived I found the entire population inside their homes behind locked doors ... I was informed that for five days no one had gone beyond their own doorsteps – the insanitary condition of the courtyard testified to the truth of this statement – that food was running short, and that the people would starve if the tiger was not killed or driven away.

Normally it was no easy matter for a District Officer to find someone who would go after a man-eating tiger. For one thing the job was dangerous, and for another it was extremely hard work, as few roads then existed, and most of the travel had to be done on foot in mountainous country. Above all, the hunter had to be both skilful and highly selective: to shoot the wrong tiger would not remove the menace.

Corbett possessed all the necessary skills in the highest degree. Besides being a first-class shot and tracker, he had exceptional patience and endurance. Once on the trail of a confirmed man-eater, he would pursue it with extraordinary dedication and disregard of hardship, often sitting up all night and walking twenty or more miles in a day. Yet if there was ever the slightest question about an animal's identify or guilt, he would give it the benefit of the doubt.

It has also been claimed, in an attempt at belittlement, that Corbett enjoyed the patronage of the Viceroys, and so could get a tiger declared a man-eater whenever he wished. This is also a *canard*, for the only Viceroy who knew him at all well (and who wrote a foreword for *Man-Eaters of Kumaon*) was Lord Linlithgow. Since he did not take office until 1936, and all but one of Jim's man-eaters had been shot by then, it is clear that Viceregal patronage was not a factor.

During the 1960s, in a fit of nationalist feeling, a move was initiated to re-name Corbett park after a leading politician, G. B. Pant, who had no connection with wildlife. Fortunately the Chairman of the State Committee concerned allowed himself to be convinced that Corbett's name should stand.

Jim Corbett was certainly a man born before his time – or maybe he was meant to show a lesser breed that an era was ending. 'As kindly and generous as he was fearless, he gave freely of himself and asked nothing in return,' wrote Lord Hailey:

I think that in the olden days he would have been one of the small band of Europeans whose memory has been worshipped by Indians as that of men who were also in some measure gods.

That seems to me a fitting epitaph. The ideas that Corbett advocated, and the books that he wrote, helped kindle a flame which still burns fitfully after these many years – and with that, I am sure, he must rest content.

4

THE TURN OF THE TIDE

The metre-gauge train squealed slowly to a halt at the wayside
station of Pallia Kalan. It was 3.30 in the morning of May 1,
1945, and after leaving the army at the end of the war I had
come to farm in North Kheri. I loaded my luggage into a
bullock cart and set off on the three-mile walk to the 750-acre
block of land which I had leased from the Government. Under
the bright stars a dog barked sleepily as we passed: the air was
still deliciously cool.

Five small villages lined a tributary of the Sarda river, but
from my land a limitless sea of grass stretched to the village of
Majhra Singahi, fourteen miles away, the western limit of the
feudal state of Singahi. The dirt-track on which I walked was
reputed to have been made for the visit of the Prince of Wales,
when he came to pig-stick in the grant belonging to the
descendants of General Sir John Hearsey, who quelled the
mutiny in Calcutta and was given land in recognition of his
service. Such imperial echoes hovered in my mind as I trudged
along.

A fox gave a chattering bark, and to the north a pack of
jackals set up their mournful chorus: *Dead Hindu! Dead Hindu!
Where are you? Where are you?* As I turned into my land the stars

were paling in the east, and from a clump of trees lining a *bhagar*, or low-lying marshy watercourse, came the guttural, sawing grunts of a leopard as he retired to his hide-out for the day.

By the time I reached my destination, the rim of the sun was showing, fiery red, and I sat down to wait for the labourers who were to build me a grass hut. As dawn broke I made out a herd of black buck, and farther away, on the horizon, a group of nilgai, India's largest antelope: the slaty-coloured bulls, much darker and larger than their beige females, with their distinctive white stockings, were already making for the shade of some acacia trees, where they planned to shelter from the summer heat.

Soon the labourers arrived, and in a very short time we had built the grass hut in which, as it turned out, I spent the next nine years. But in my new-found keenness to get things done I went down with a severe attack of sunstroke. As I tossed restlessly under a straw roof, the heat seemed unendurable, but when I did as the local people suggested and took frequent drinks of salted mango-juice, I was soon on my feet again.

The sowing of farm crops pitched me into conflict with the ubiquitous wild pigs, who at that stage competed successfully with humans in making a living off the land. Maize, wheat and paddy (rice) were all grist to their voracious appetite, and they lived and bred outrageously in fields of sugar-cane. It was memorable, if infuriating, to walk through a field at night and hear the brittle crack of each individually-nurtured cane-stick — a sound that seemed to the overburdened farmer like the breaking of his own bones.

Often, while still in college before the war, I had heard of the wildlife of Kheri, and in particular of the swamp deer, which lived by the thousand in the catchment area of the Sarda river. I had heard how the rulers of Singahi used to invite dignitaries of the Raj to shoot the deer, and how Kanwar Dilipat Shah, of the ruling family, was supposed to be the best running game-shot in the world.

The great herds of deer were driven galloping past butts by beaters mounted on elephants, and in a single day as many as thirty or forty master stags would be mown down. All the

hunters wanted was their antlers: the heads were cut off for trophies, and the carcases left to scavengers.

Among the Raja of Singahi's relations was the Maharaj
Kumar of Vizianagram, a leading patron of cricket, known as
'Vizzy', who once invited the M.C.C. to play a match against a
home team, and then took the captain, D. R. Jardine, to hunt in
the preserves of Singahi. The party shot five tigers near Majhra
Singahi.

Such was the fame of Kheri's wildlife. For my first two years in
the area I was too busy to look far beyond the land I was working,
and although there were plenty of animals in the immediate
vicinity, I saw no tigers. Then, after the holocaust brought
about by the partition of the sub-continent into India and Pakistan, large numbers of displaced Sikh farmers came looking for
land. The rulers of Singahi, already threatened by the central
government with the abolition of their feudal rights and with
appropriation of their surplus land, hastily began to lease blocks
to the new arrivals, rather than wait for the Government to take
over the land for a nominal amount.

Soon all the grassland to the west of my block had been let to
displaced farmers from the Punjab. The newcomers found it a
struggle to adapt to their new environment: they had exchanged
the dry heat of their homeland for the humid and enervating
climate of the Terai, whose native people had always lived at
subsistence level, rendered ambitionless by seasonal fevers and
the raids of crop-eating animals and the dacoits, or bandits, who
sheltered in the forests. The colonising farmers soon showed
they were made of sterner stuff: though plagued at first by
malaria, which killed quite a few of them, they hung on grimly
and began to make a decent living, their ambition succeeding
where the apathy of the locals had failed.

As farms began to open up the grassland all round me, I conceived the idea of buying a crawler tractor and accelerating the
work. I also hoped to pay for the tractor by ploughing for other
farmers on contract. Having always been an admirer of sheer
physical force, I was fascinated to watch the plough cutting into
the land with apparently effortless ease. In the overturned
furrows of virgin soil there kept appearing writhing portions of
great snakes, sliced to pieces as they sheltered underground.

I also took my tractor to the famous Mirchia jheel, renowned as the optimum habitat of the swamp deer herds. In my imagination the marshes still seemed to stink of bygone slaughter, and I saw only one hind splashing through a distant patch of water, while farther to the north a flock of mallard rose to the boom of a muzzle-loading musket.

Then, as sunset lights were burning low across the marsh, I heard a thrilling sound. For a moment the deep, monosyllabic *aoom*! seemed to hold the rays of the departing sun suspended: it swelled like the note of an organ in some great cathedral, then died away. Once more came that resonant *aoom*! It was the King of the Jungle, proclaiming his sway. But no alarm calls from subject animals answered in homage; only the spiralling smoke from innumerable wood fires showed that the invasion of his kingdom had already begun.

A few days later, along the track leading from my farm to the main road, I came on the pug-marks of a tigress approaching my hutment. My first reaction was one of joy that the legendary predator had come to share living space with me. What I failed to realise was that I myself had set off the process of attrition which was going to clear the tigers' age-old home and force them to disperse. The animal which had always shunned humans was now being forced to come to terms with his oppressor.

The land between Pallia and Majhra Singahi is sandy, so that the grass which grew on it was not tall enough to provide tigers with a comfortable habitat, and in any case the presence of the occasional human was enough to keep them away. Immediately to the north, just short of the Nepalese border, were luxuriant stands of ratwa grass, interspersed with low-lying marshes and great patches of narkul reeds, which formed ideal tiger territory. Better still, there was a plentiful supply of prey animals, and a virulent form of malaria had until then prevented encroachment by humans. Yet already this little patch of tiger paradise was changing, for as a result of reclamation work even the Mirchia jheel and its adjoining marshes had begun to silt up.

The next serious blow was struck in the 1950s, when the Central Government launched a scheme to hand over the land already appropriated by the abolition of feudal rights to destitute labourers from the eastern part of the state. The area selected for this operation was around Majhra Singahi and Khajuria, and had been some of the best tiger country outside the reserved forest. Inevitably there now occurred the first clashes in our area between tigers and men.

The first human victim was a boy who happened to go and cut grass on the very spot in which a tiger had chosen to lie up for the day. His death was an accident, pure and simple, for the tiger which killed him was quite normal. Next, a tigress began to eat people, and when she was shot it was found that her jaw had been broken by a poacher's slug, and had calloused over so that she could not use her canines properly. Then another old tigress took to man-eating: forced to live in an area surrounded by humans, she had adopted them as a prey-species.

I myself was asked to destroy these three animals; and, not having attained much maturity of thought, I did it without great compunction. In fact for a short time I even nursed an ambition to become the Jim Corbett of Kheri. Soon, I am glad to say, I abandoned any such idea, for I saw all too clearly that the dice of fortune were heavily loaded against the tiger, and that I was morally bound to support him, rather than help in his extermination.

At about this time there occurred an extraordinary incident, reminiscent of the occasion on which the Victorian 'Felix' shot the caged panther. One day the Divisional Commissioner – an officer of the Indian Civil Service – came to visit the colonists in Kheri. Someone had netted a crocodile, and the creature was brought to the Commissioner with the servile suggestion that he might like to shoot it – whereupon he loaded his rifle and did just that, the poor crocodile still being enmeshed in the net. No doubt the man had the skin made up into a suitcase and a pair of shoes.

After the three clashes during the colonisation scheme, there followed a long and deceptive lull of nearly twenty years, during which the tigers adapted themselves to live in closer proximity to man, and no further fatalities took place – at least on the human side. One reason for the respite was that although much of the virgin land had been cultivated, the tall grass had been replaced by an alternative form of cover almost equally well-suited to tigers – sugar-cane, which grows to a height of ten or twelve feet, and offers dense, quiet shelter through the winter months. Tigers which spilled over out of the forest, when populations there became too high, lived and bred in the sugar-cane and in marshes, and lived on the wild pig and deer which themselves subsisted on the farm crops.

At first this new arrangement seemed to work and the tiger was actually regarded as a benefactor. I remember being told by farmers whose land my tractor had ploughed that the tiger was the best unpaid nightwatchman they had, for on any night that one passed through their fields, no animals came to eat the crops.

Nevertheless, violent encounters with tigers still took place. One night, within a mile of my farm, some locals set up a series of nets, into which they planned to drive the marauding wild pigs. (This was a very cruel method of killing them, as any pig caught would be beaten to death with sticks, and the poor animal might be belaboured, shrieking and squealing, for hours before it expired.) That night, however, the victim was more formidable than anyone expected: the animal caught was a tiger, and as no one had the courage to approach him, he eventually bit his way out. Another night a tiger was caught in a gin trap set for deer. This time the trappers approached the struggling tiger with spears, but after they had stuck him in the rump several times the pain-maddened animal pulled free and killed two of his tormentors.

The more securely the farmers established themselves, the greater the inroads they began to make on the stock of wild ungulates. The shooting of deer, done in the name of crop-protection, became in fact a profitable sideline: antlers and flesh were sold in local markets, and the number of deer started to fall.

The decline put the tigers into much more direct conflict with the human invaders. First they began to take domestic buffaloes and cattle; then they were compelled to prey on species with which they would not naturally bother – dogs, goats and even chickens. This ludicrous state of affairs could not continue for long, and tigresses with suckling cubs, living in sugar-cane patches, were driven by necessity to accept the human being as prey.

All this time, tigers were still being shot: some in the reserved forest, where blocks were allocated by ballot and only one tiger was allowed to be killed at a time, and others out in the farm land. It is hard to say which form of shooting was more pernicious, for both in a way were big business.

That in the forest was mostly organised by the shikar outfitters – professional firms who brought in paying clients from abroad to shoot big game. On the pseudo-patriotic pretext of earning much-needed foreign exchange, the shikar companies ignored the danger signals, and were prepared to slaughter tigers to the bitter end, the final bloodstained dollar. Their clients, far from showing concern at the plight of their quarry, described their exploits in language no less melodramatic and overwrought than that used by Captain Shakespear a century before. One of them, the American Denton Scott, could still write in 1960:

We were in a lost position, almost a 100 yards from the tree and the safety of the machan. In a few quick bounds the tiger could be among us, sweeping his great paws. It would have to be one shot, and it would have to kill him – dead. Or else we would be. Now suddenly the three of us had rifles to our shoulders. It was a long shot, at least three hundred yards. I had no scope on the ·458 and all I could see clearly was his great head ... Now we knew how death in the jungle arrived, silently, deadly, without warning. We had been coldly close to it in those few minutes.

As the years passed, I myself grew restive. My farm was no longer surrounded by virgin grassland: in every direction the chequerboard of new fields stretched to the horizon, and the wild animals had vanished almost as completely as the original landscape. I became determined to find another home, further from the steamroller of civilisation, and thus it was that in 1959 I moved a few miles northwards and settled on the edge of the jungle. In my earlier books I have described how I built first a shack and then a permanent house, which I called Tiger Haven, on the bank of a small river, with the jungle towering directly behind it on an escarpment. Suffice it to say here that my new home put me back in close contact with wild animals, and in particular with leopards and tigers, which lived in the forest behind the house. The one serious drawback of the place, as I soon discovered, was that during the monsoon months of July, August, September and October it becomes completely cut off by water, as the rivers, swollen by torrential rains both locally and in the hills of Nepal, burst their banks and flood all the land roundabout.

At first, having cleared some land, I tried to grow normal farm crops; but gradually my interest in agriculture gave way to a passion for the study and conservation of wildlife. I still cultivated a few acres, but the crops I sowed were put in purely for the benefit of the deer, and I spent more and more of my time patrolling the jungle tracks in search of the pug-marks, scrapes and droppings which gave clues about the great cats' habits.

It took me several years to acquire a thorough knowledge of even the relatively small patch of jungle within walking-distance of Tiger Haven: at first I was often lost, confused by the similarity of different paths and blocks of forest, and I was amazed at the ease with which the animals found their own way round. Clearly tigers and leopards carry much more complex information in their heads than they are generally given credit for.

In this context I have been much struck by the work of the South African writer André Marais, who conducted some fascinating experiments in direction-finding. In one, six trained trackers, together with a pack-horse, trekked 200 miles from A to B, blazing a trail as they went. After they had reached their destination heavy rain washed out all the signs they had left along the route, and none of them could retrace it. The one member of the party able to find his way back was the horse, who not only led the way but stopped at each of the camp-sites. Another experiment showed that a man's direction-finding instincts, normally submerged, surfaced and worked efficiently under hypnosis – and I am certain that most wild animals have powers in this field which humans have suppressed.

As time went on, I gradually built up a map of the Tiger Haven area, adding names of my own to the few that already existed. These new place-names nearly all came from the operations of myself and my staff: either we built a machan (tree-platform) at a suitable site, or some event occurred by which a particular spot could be remembered. Thus Tiger Well, Leopard Haven, Juliette Point and many others all became well-known to us, but would have meant nothing to strangers.

From the number of place-names on the map at each end of the book, readers might get an impression of a well-populated area, but this would be very misleading. The one settlement of any size is Dudhwa – then a forest rest house and camp, and now the headquarters of the Dudhwa National Park. Apart from this, the only inhabited places are the other rest houses such as Sathiana.

The Soheli river, running roughly from west to east in this area, is the natural boundary of the forest. South of it is a belt of grass, and then farm land. North of it there is jungle: jamun and other wet-land trees by the river, and, on the escarpment above, sal, teak and other hardwoods. The only metalled road is the one from Pallia to Dudhwa and Gauriphanta; the other roads are all made of earth, and have to be rebuilt after every monsoon, for the floods sweep some parts of them away and block others with deposits of silt. Because the area has plenty of dense cover and carries a good stock of prey species – mainly chital, swamp deer, sambar, hog deer and wild pigs – it is prime tiger habitat.

As soon as I began to study tigers in earnest, I took to baiting them – that is, staking out baits such as domestic buffaloes at selected sites in the jungle. The aim of this process is three-fold: first, to draw tigers into a particular area, or hold them in it if they are already there; second, to take the pressure off wild prey populations; and third, to bring the tigers to a spot at which one can watch them from a specially-built machan or other vantage point. In times of scarcity baiting can also be used to help tigers through a lean period.

Many people who have never seen it believe that the use of live animals as bait is cruel. But anyone who knows how most Indians treat animals at once acknowledges that it is far better for a buffalo to be killed by a tiger than – the usual alternatives – to be worked or beaten to death, or slaughtered by a Muhammadan butcher, or Hindu swineherd.

Western travellers are often appalled by the callous indifference displayed by Indians towards animals. If a sacred cow, for instance, is hurt in a traffic accident, it may lie in the road for days, perhaps with a broken back, until it dies from thirst, pain and exhaustion. Nobody is prepared to mercy-kill it, still less to do anything about rescuing it.

A butcher's traditional method of slaughter is no less cruel or primitive: he knocks the fully-conscious animal to the ground, drops on it astride its neck, and invokes the name of the Almighty three times before sawing at its throat with a knife, usually coated in rust. Often he does not reach the jugular artery first time, and the wretched beast squirms to its death in a welter of blood and imprecations.

The slaughter of pigs is still more barbaric. In my part of India they are killed only by members of a particular caste, the Khatiks, who force the animal into a narrow kind of crush, with barred sides. The executioner then attempts to drive a pointed piece of metal or a fire-hardened stake into its heart, between the slats, but often the pig is stuck in the stomach, intestines or neck, and sometimes it escapes altogether, to die days later.

A tiger, by contrast, approaches silently and kills quickly, often in only a few seconds, for his very existence depends on his ability to do just this. Evolution has made him a killing-instrument of the utmost efficiency, and his entire existence revolves round the imperative of hunting. His aim is to satisfy his hunger with the least possible effort.

There is a world of difference between the still greenery of the jungle and the frantic scramble of a slaughter-yard. Even a buffalo – supposedly one of the stupidest animals – smells the blood, senses the stress and becomes highly nervous when it goes to a butcher. A bait tied out on a kill-site, by contrast, lies down and chews its cud, perfectly calm.

There is one other point in favour of being killed by the tiger. As everyone knows who has been hurt in an accident, shock anaesthetises: for a few minutes after being injured you feel no pain. The Victorian accounts of tiger-hunting contain many instances of men being savaged by animals, but in every one the message is the same: the victim felt nothing until later.

One such was Captain Glasfurd. When savaged by a bear which he had flushed out of a cave, he felt absolutely no sense of pain, and it was therefore with a kind of 'humorous incredulity' that he found his breeches soaked in blood and his right leg punctured by holes big enough to admit his fingers – 'the injuries being such as would call up feelings of sickening apprehension if viewed inflicted on another person'. Gordon Cumming had a similar experience, also when attacked by a bear:

As I fended her off with my left arm, she got it in her mouth and crunched it up like a cucumber . . . My left wrist was nearly bitten through, both bones were smashed, and the hand twisted round . . . I was astonished at the utter absence of pain, for the wound was gruesome to behold.

Clearly, the same applies to victims of the great cats. The explorer David Livingstone was mauled by a lion, and A. W. Strachan of the Indian Police lost his leg to a tiger – yet neither felt anything at the time. Before an animal attacked by a tiger can feel pain, it is dead. I therefore consider live baiting to be fully justified – especially as all it does, in effect, is to swap one victim for another. The tiger must kill anyway. Once when I was discussing the subject with the Prime Minister, Mrs Gandhi, and she maintained that the practice was cruel, I said to her, 'Madam – your butcher kills for you,' and she answered, 'Yes – I suppose that's right.'

Spending much time in the jungle, both at night and by day, I witnessed at first hand the decline in predator populations. When I first settled at Tiger Haven there were three leopards living in my immediate neighbourhood. Although I rarely saw them, I frequently found their pug-marks close to the house, showing where they had passed during their nocturnal journeys, and at night I would hear their sawing grunts. Yet with the price of skins at an all-time high, every poacher in the district was after them, and within a few years they had vanished.

The tigers were much better established, and their very numbers tended to keep the leopards away – for the secondary predators always avoid the presence of their senior cousins. One reason for the tigers' success was that the habitat suited them particularly well; but the main factor was that their numbers had been artificially boosted by an influx of animals over the border from Nepal. There, too, profound changes had taken place over the past decade, and although the causes were different, the result was much the same.

In 1950 a popular revolt swept away the corrupt old Rana regime, which had ruled Nepal despotically for a hundred years. The era of the great tiger-shoots ended – but so did the age-old protection of the forests which the Ranas' enthusiasm for hunting had ensured. In the preceding few years the human population had grown so much that the mountains could no longer support all the people trying to live there, and thousands were forced down to the lower ground such as the valley of Chitwan in a desperate search for new land. For centuries the dreaded scourge of *awal*, or endemic malaria, had helped keep humans at bay; but now a huge mosquito-eradication pro-gramme proved so successful that people became able to live in, and destroy, the tigers' ancestral breeding grounds. Many tigers, fleeing before this mass-attack on Nepal's forests, crossed over into India and created a temporary, illusory surplus in northern areas.

Even so, it was a heartbreaking business to make the acquaintance of individual tigers in my own area, to watch them, feed them with domestic buffaloes, protect them – and then see them gunned down by the still-legitimate expeditions organised by the shikar outfitters. In one of the most disastrous local massacres, which took place in April 1969, a party of Americans camping at Sathiana shot three of my old friends – the Red Tiger, the Black Tiger, and the old, lame tiger with a twisted foot – and then moved on amid scenes of great jubilation to the Fort Block, east of Tiger Haven, where they slaughtered two more. People like this paid enormous sums to kill a tiger and take away its skin, often arriving at their shooting-camp and departing again within twenty-four hours: 3,000 dollars was no unusual price for a single animal, and some people paid up to 10,000.

The tiger had become the major hunting trophy in the world. Knowing, as I did, that the events in my patch of jungle were being repeated in dozens of other places, I became more and more depressed.

Then, at this low point, there shone out one ray of light: the publication of a book called *The Deer and the Tiger* by the outstanding American naturalist George Schaller. Before coming to India, Schaller had completed a two-year study of the mountain gorilla in Africa. In this he established that the tales of the animal's innate savagery, brought back by the nineteenth-century French explorer du Chaillu and others such as R. M. Ballantyne, were quite untrue, and that the gorilla, in spite of its colossal strength, was a perfectly peaceful creature, which had accepted him, the human intruder, into its own environment.

In 1965 Schaller turned his attention to tigers, and for thirteen months he lived among them in the Kanha National Park, in Madhya Pradesh. Unarmed and on foot, he followed them and their prey about their daily business – and he came to conclusions similar to those of Jim Corbett. Tigers (he wrote) are 'on the whole very good tempered,' and far from the bloodthirsty aggressors depicted by Captain Shakespear and his kind:

The tiger's reputation for savagery appears to be based largely upon its capacity to do harm, and on the fact that ... when shot and only wounded it may attack and kill the careless hunter. Exaggerated accounts by hunters have added to the widespread misconception about the cats' response to man.

Schaller knew what he was writing about, for in the course of his study he had many close confrontations, but only once found himself obliged to climb a tree, after he had almost walked on top of a sleeping tigress. The most 'vigorous response' he got was from a tigress with a single cub, whom he had followed as she dragged her kill over a ridge and through a dry stream-bed. When Schaller sat down on a boulder, at the edge of a patch of tall grass surrounded by bamboo, where he hoped the tigress might be, he was rewarded by a low continuous growling:

The tigress rose 120 feet away and pulled the corners of her mouth back in a snarl several times. Suddenly she bounded fifty feet towards me, emitting two coughing roars. She then retreated seventy feet and for twenty minutes crouched, only part of her face showing. Finally she departed with her cub.

In general, he found the tigers of Kanha extraordinarily retiring. He realised that they were probably more tolerant of humans than others elsewhere, for in the National Park they had not been shot at or otherwise harassed since 1952; yet, even allowing for this local difference of behaviour, he made out a convincing case when he described tigers as animals which 'are generally so shy, and avoid man so assiduously, that they are rarely seen'.

Schaller's clarion call of good sense and observation, of detailed scientific study tempered by human understanding, came out at a most opportune moment. Yet by the time *The Deer and the Tiger* was published, the situation was so far gone that no single book, however excellent, could hope to arrest the decline: habitat was being destroyed at an unprecedented rate, and tigers were still being shot.

The shooting in the forest was allocated by a system of ballot, and each person who drew lucky was allowed only one animal. To circumvent this restriction, one unsavoury pair of sportsmen took to going after farm tigers, on which there was then no limit. After they had destroyed a few, I approached the Chief Wildlife Warden of the area, who was supposed to be protecting animals, and proposed to him that we should bring a court case against the two men, to stop the pointless slaughter.

The Chief Wildlife Warden agreed; and so, the next time the men shot a tiger in the fields, we worked up a case against them. Unfortunately, at the last moment, no official could be found to give evidence, and as a result I and my native tracker, Jackson, had to appear in court in an attempt to lend veracity to the prosecution. Although the case failed, it had the salutary effect of putting an end to that particular form of shooting, and gave the local tigers a respite.

Straightforward poaching was less easy to control. Everyone was after tigers for their skins, which were fetching high prices in foreign markets, and in my part of the country the trade was made easier by the fact that the Nepalese frontier, unsealed and unguarded, was only a mile or two away. Once across the grassy track that marked the border, a skin could be disposed of with no questions asked.

Among the last of the native tiger-slayers was Vizzy, the Maharaj Kumar of Vizianagram. During the late 1960s, with his own score approaching the 400 mark, he returned to his old stamping-grounds of Majhra Singahi, by then renamed Sampurnagar in honour of a Chief Minister of Uttar Pradesh. Although he had been nominated Vice-Chairman of the State Board for Wildlife, his conscience permitted him the luxury of a tiger-shoot on an old-fashioned scale. The marshes and stands of narkul had given way to sugar-cane, but the tigers were still there. During a beat Vizzy fired at and wounded a tigress, who took refuge in a field of sugar-cane, only to charge out at the rifleman's elephant, which bolted. Vizzy was thrown off, damaging a kidney and possibly other internal organs, for he did not survive long; and with his passing the sport-killing of tigers came to an end.

Destructive though the shooting was, by far the greatest threat to tigers' survival was the erosion of their habitat. Just as the grasslands of North Kheri had been swept away by the plough, so forests all over the sub-continent were plundered for timber on a scale never known before. Thousands of acres were felled indiscriminately in search of quick profits, and thousands more infiltrated by villagers living round the edges of the jungle, who allowed their animals to graze in the forest, and who cut firewood illegally. By this kind of insidious, creeping take-over, vast areas were swiftly eroded.

From now on it became increasingly difficult for a tiger to find a habitat that suited him. Instead, he often had to travel long distances in search of a comfortable niche – for tigers are solitary animals, and strongly territorial, and a resident male rarely welcomes a vagrant to his patch on any permanent basis. The planting of extensive sugar-cane crops did provide extra habitat around some forests, but the innovation was potentially dangerous, in that, by making tigers too tolerant of human presence, it increased the chance of clashes between one species and the other.

The great cats of India reached their lowest ebb in 1969. Tigers were still not officially in danger of extinction, for they were not listed in the International Union for the Conservation of Nature's Red Books, which record all threatened species. Twenty-six licensed shikar firms were still operating in India, all ostensibly to earn foreign exchange for the country. Most of them were well-financed and highly-organised; as their expertise increased, and at the same time habitat shrank, the pressure on the remaining tigers became unbearable.

Help finally arrived at the Tenth General Assembly of the I.U.C.N., which was held in Delhi during November 1969. The Prime Minister, in her speech welcoming the delegates, admitted the need for foreign exchange, but disclaimed any desire to earn it at the expense of our tigers. Finding an overwhelming sympathy for the plight of the tiger among almost everyone present, I submitted a paper suggesting a ban on tiger-shooting, and this, to my great relief, was accepted as the epoch-making Resolution No. 16:

In view of the grave threat to the tiger-populations in the countries where the animal occurs, due to direct and indirect methods of destruction such as licensed hunting, poisoning, burning of breeding cover, destruction of habitat, and biotic activities such as grazing and the skin and fur trade, the Tenth General Assembly of the I.U.C.N. meeting at New Delhi in 1969 –

*Recommends to these countries the declaration of a moratorium on the killing of this animal until such time as censuses and ecological studies, which are in operation or are proposed, are completed and reveal the correct position as regards population trends.

*Further recommends that the tourist and economic contribution of the tiger be shifted from the killing by a few commercial hunters to enable it to be watched and photographed wild in sanctuaries and national parks for the benefit of many.

*Expresses satisfaction that the export of tiger and leopard skins has been forbidden, but regrets to find an open sale for tiger skins, and other trophies and articles, and requests the Government of India to take measures to close any remaining loopholes either in the scope or enforcement of the relevant legal restrictions.

Typically, the only people who opposed the resolution were my fellow Indians, but in spite of their obstruction it was passed. The spokesman for the tiger protection lobby, K. S. Sankhala (then Director of Delhi Zoo), called on Mrs Gandhi to give tigers immediate protection.

This her Government did, first by ordering State administrations to make their own arrangements for the local safeguarding of tigers, and then by passing a law which banned all tiger-hunting. Needless to say, the shikar firms were aghast. One outfitter sent a circular letter to its numerous clients asking them all to write to the Government of India and point out the financial loss which the country would suffer, as well as to claim that the commercial hunting firms were the best preservationists, as they would never kill the geese that laid golden eggs for them. Another company maintained that poachers would move in if they were forced out. (This, they knew, was quite unrealistic, for although poachers armed with primitive weapons have the fire-power to kill leopards, they rarely have the full-bore rifles needed to take on a tiger. Besides as two tigers had recently been found dead in a block which paying clients had been shooting, it was hard to say who would be more lethal: the shikar firm itself, or hypothetical poachers.) Yet another company, headed by 'Tootoo' Imam, a notorious opponent of conservation tried a different ploy and wrote to the Prime Minister pointing out that since tigers cost poor cultivators sixty million rupees a year in lost livestock, they should be preserved only in zoos. To cap everything the Shikar Outfitters' Association had the effrontery to lodge an appeal in the High Court claiming loss of livelihood, but fortunately it was rejected.

Gradually the furore died down. Instead of putting their resources into wildlife tourism – as they had been invited to do by the Government Tourist Department – the outfitters who had recently professed such concern about the tiger's future opened cinemas or moved into other rewarding business ventures.

The lead taken by India soon had wider repercussions. Other countries began to introduce similar bans, and the distinguished British naturalist Guy Mountfort urged the World Wildlife Fund to raise money by mounting an international campaign. First, however, more accurate information was needed about the actual number of tigers remaining – and when it came, it brought a severe shock. A survey carried out by the Indian Department of Forests under the direction of S. R. Choudhury showed that in the whole of the sub-continent fewer than 2,000 tigers were left. Nobody could be sure how accurate the survey was, but a careful record of pug-marks, droppings, calls, kills, and sightings produced a total of 1,827, plus or minus ten per cent. Of a population once estimated at 40,000, less than five per cent remained. Nobody could now doubt that the Indian tiger was on its way out.

Galvanised by this disastrous information, Mountfort flew to Delhi and, with colleagues from the World Wildlife Fund, interviewed Mrs Gandhi. He proposed that if India would set aside a number of reserves, the I.U.C.N. should draw up proposals for their scientific management, and the World Wildlife Fund would raise a million dollars to finance the rescue operation. The Prime Minister's response was gratifyingly swift: she immediately agreed to form a Tiger Task Force, and proved as good as her word by appointing the first members of the body the very next day.

In 1972 the Government passed the Indian Wildlife Act, which at last set realistic schedules and penalties, and in September of that year the World Wildlife Fund launched Operation Tiger, its fund-raising scheme. Such was the enthusiasm generated that in only eighteen months the campaign collected no less than 1,750,000 dollars. Nor was the benefit purely financial: the interest created by the fund-raising activities brought about a world-wide realignment of people's ideas about tigers. Suddenly everyone was tiger-conscious. Just as in London a tiger-skin coat was symbolically burnt in protest, so the International Fur Trades Federation banned the importation of tiger-skins. The greatest single advance, however, was the international treaty, drawn up by the I.U.C.N., which made it illegal to export or import any animal listed as endangered in the Red Books, or to deal in their skins. By the time over fifty nations had ratified this treaty, the legal trade in tiger-skins dwindled almost to nothing.

Above *Safe on elephants, Victorian hunters score again*
Below *Viceregal slaughter: Lord Reading and his bag*

Left *Legendary hunter: Jim Corbett in 1938*

Below *Lord Curzon with the Maharaja of Rewa*

No praise can be too high for the idealism and energy with which the officials of the World Wildlife Fund, particularly Guy Mountfort, launched this great drive. It was undoubtedly the international response which turned the tiger back from the brink of extinction.

In India itself, things at first moved with equal despatch. The rescue plan, which came to be known as Project Tiger, was launched in 1972, with a six-year budget of almost six million dollars. The first Director was K. S. Sankhala, and work began at once. Unfortunately a serious mistake was made in designating, for the first tiger reserves, areas in which the animals were already well established, such as Corbett, Kanha and Ranthambore. It would have been much better to set aside other, more vulnerable areas, in which the population was at greater risk.

At all events, in the core areas of the forests designated as tiger reserves commercial production of timber ceased. Vehicles, boats and radios were bought, and a start made on the formidable job of training Forest Department Staff to look after wildlife rather than timber and other forest produce.

No one will deny that in the twelve years since Project Tiger was launched significant progress has been made. India now has thirteen tiger reserves; the tiger population has stabilised and started to grow again. The tiger has become our national animal, symbol not only of all India's wildlife, but of the conservation effort as a whole.

Yet at the same time the conservation programme has thrown up many severe problems, not least an outbreak of man-eating on an unprecedented scale. If man has saved the tiger temporarily, he has also thrown himself into head-on confrontation with it, and it is the difficulties and dangers of the confrontation that I wish to examine in the second part of this book.

5

TIGER BEHAVIOUR

It may be useful at this stage to include a brief account of tiger behaviour – although it must be remembered that different environments condition behaviour in many ways, and also that the characters of individual tigers vary as much as those of humans.

The tiger is a solitary, heavily-armed predator with ultra-fast reactions, and lives in a habitat of restricted vision. From these facts flow certain consequences. One is that he must have an efficient system of communication, to avoid sudden confrontations with other tigers. Since almost anything that moves in the jungle is potential prey, and since abrupt movements trigger the attack reflex, an unexpected meeting with another tiger may lead to an instantaneous and possibly fatal clash. Therefore he has highly acute senses. His ears are as sharp as those of any animal, and his eyes are the brightest of any creature on earth: if seen at dusk, or after dark in the beam of a lamp, they blaze back the ambient light with awe-inspiring intensity.

The tiger's nose, too, though often denigrated, is of vital importance to him. Most books are at pains to point out that a tiger's power of scent is practically non-existent: authors base this theory on the way some animal has approached a kill and been shot, without realising that a human is sitting up in wait, or on other superficial checks in which captive tigers – whose sensory powers are in any case degraded – have been unable to smell out highly-scented meat.

According to my own observations over a number of years, especially of the group among whom I lived for seventeen months, tigers make extensive use of their noses while moving through the jungle, and they are constantly picking up messages left by members of their own and other species. Strong smells invariably provoke the grimace known by the German name of *Flehmen*, in which the nose is wrinkled and the tongue allowed to protrude, and there is no doubt that tigers can follow the scent left by a drag indefinitely. If they sometimes seem to ignore the scent signals which they pick up from the environment, it may be that they are relying on information from the other senses as well, or simply that they have the confidence to disregard obvious danger signs – for even man is not an inveterate enemy.

The principal method of message-leaving is spraying – the discharge of a mixture of scent (from the anal glands under the tail) and urine against a convenient tree or rock. It is done by both sexes, but the spray of the female is more diffuse and may be less pungent than that of the male. Broadly speaking, its purpose is to attract the opposite sex by advertising sexual condition (as when the female is in season) or to act as a warning signal to animals of the same sex. As one spray may remain detectable for as long as a month, it conveys information not only about what animal has passed, but also about when it passed, and so can act as a spacing-mechanism. Spraying is probably the most effective and widely-used means of communication between tigers; but sometimes it indicates a release of tension, and it is also apparently used for way-marking and direction-finding – as for instance when a tigress has moved her cubs to some new base, or intends moving, and marks the route to it.

Another form of communication is the scrape, in which the animal gouges the ground hard with one hind paw after the other, claws unsheathed. After this it may defecate or urinate on the scrapes, or deposit a token amount of either function, or leave the marks bare. Depending on the size of the tiger, the scrapes may be up to eighteen inches long and three deep. Scraping is clearly a ritual activity, quite separate from the natural processes of elimination, and it is used mainly by dominant animals, usually males, to announce their occupation of a range; it thus prevents chance encounters in territory that may be temporarily overcrowded.

A less obvious ploy is the scraping of claws down the bark of trees. The same tree, once chosen, is used continually, and large tigers score deep longitudinal cuts down the bark. Claw segments are frequently found embedded in the bark, so it seems that the practice helps with claw-cleaning; and as scraping trees are often found near kill-sites, they probably also mark the centre of a range.

Tigers are normally silent animals, though they have a greater range of calls than leopards. Captive tiger cubs have often been heard to call their mothers with a falsetto *ah-ah*, and they also use this call on their human keepers, of whom they become extremely fond. Communication from mother to cub is effected either by direct calls or by example, which the offspring are always quick to follow.

All adult tigers use the greeting known as *Prusten* – a friendly, fluttering exhalation made through closed lips. Less easy to interpret is *pooking*, which resembles the call of a sambar. This has been much discussed and variously interpreted as a sex call, a contact call, and even as a decoy call to lure the deer to its doom. I myself, having heard a tigress use it when leading her cubs to kill in the presence of other tigers, and having known the same tigress use it to summon her cubs after she had demonstrated against me, believe that it must be a contact call tempered with suspicion. Schaller lends support to this theory with his report that pooking has been associated with scent-marking and urination, both advertisement devices.

The tiger's loudest and most stirring call is his resonant *aoom!*, which echoes through the jungle for up to a mile. Sometimes it is used to make contact with another tiger, and sometimes as a warning, to clear the way ahead of possible intruders. Calls vary in intensity and volume according to the message they carry, and obviously one tiger's voice differs from that of another. Even a human can often tell the difference. In due course I have come to be able to recognise four or five different tigers at any one time from the pitch of their voices.

As a further means of avoiding encounters in a crowded space – particularly at a kill-site – males use moaning and roaring, again with varying intensity. A really angry tiger gives vent to the most blood-curdling roars. Other miscellaneous calls include hissing and spitting – both done when the animal objects to something which it does not like but equally does not understand, such as the flash of a camera bulb at night. Low-intensity growling usually constitutes a form of warning, telling an intruder to keep his distance or face the consequences. Often one form of call merges into another as the situation changes, but whenever he can the tiger remains silent, for his real interest lies in preserving his solitary status.

Tigers generally lie up by day, and spend most of their nights hunting. Their technique is to make a careful stalk or lie in ambush, and then attack with a short, sharp charge. Many people believe that they kill easily, but in fact they are hard put to it to kill often enough to be able to feed every day, especially a tigress with cubs. The wild game which they normally hunt has faculties attuned to self-preservation, and it is estimated that only about one tiger attack in twenty is successful. Judging from the evidence which I find of abortive attacks, where the hoof-marks of deer, deeply indented in mud, are overlaid with the claw-marks of a tiger charging, I should say that this estimate is fair enough.

The tiger, in his position as master-predator, can prey on all other species, including the calves of elephants and rhino. Corbett mentions a full-grown bull-elephant being killed by a pair of tigers at Tanakpur, in Uttar Pradesh, but this must have been an exception. Though tigers do have favourite prey species – notably swamp deer, chital and wild pig – necessity will compel them to subsist on such lowly fare as fish and frogs. They will also eat carrion in an advanced state of decomposition, and cases of cannibalism are not unknown, though only when tigers come across an animal already dead.

The tiger's killing-technique has been endlessly debated; but, having examined countless kills of both tied-up and free-running prey, I cannot agree with the conventional opinion that the tiger's aim is to break its victim's neck. Obviously, with free-running prey, no set-piece attack is possible: tactics have to be modified according to circumstances. To work out a series of permutations whose ultimate aim was to dislocate the spinal vertebrae would introduce unnecessary complications into an operation which must be as fast and simple as possible.

The ultimate target is always the neck – the most vulnerable area – and the tiger's approach to it depends on various factors: the relative positions of attacker and quarry, the evasive action taken by the victim, its size and possible means of retaliation. A tiger has a strong instinct for self-preservation, and avoids danger as much as possible. Thus if the prey animal is larger than the attacker, or has large horns, the target is usually the throat: a grip of the windpipe leads to strangulation. If the animal is the same size as the tiger or smaller, the most expedient grip is the nape-bite, which crushes the vertebrae and brings death instantaneously.

With free-running prey, the first essential is to make contact, and the tiger may hook his claws into the animal's hide or round one of its legs to bring it down before anchoring it with a nape- or throat-grip. Against an animal more or less his size he may also use a side-grip, like the hold adopted by a tigress to carry a cub. Any dislocation of the neck is fortuitous, and due to the animal falling in a particular attitude, rather than to any intentional leverage.

With tied-up baits, if the neck is broken, it happens in the fall of the victim, whose foreleg is usually tethered to a stake. The tiger uses the same grips – nape and throat, principally – but the attack is more inclined to take the form of a set-piece, if only because the target is always stationary.

The range occupied by a male tiger is estimated at between twenty-five and thirty square miles. Within each range there prevails a loose hegemony consisting of the resident male and a number of females, backed up by the younger, lesser tigers who have no land tenure of their own. Within a range the tigers are well acquainted with local conditions and with the places at which prey animals tend to collect. Ranges are not exclusive, and, provided prey is abundant, the resident male is fairly tolerant of transient junior males, whom he will allow to share kills on occasion.

The range of a tigress is a good deal smaller, mainly because of her different biological function: whenever she has young cubs, they tie her down to a relatively confined area. Again, the range is not exclusive: several females share the overlap, but they use the same spacing mechanisms as males to avoid unexpected confrontations, spraying, scraping and calling. Schaller, studying a tigress and her four cubs, estimated their range at twenty-five square miles – but the size of a territory must obviously depend on factors such as the nature of the habitat, the amount of prey available, the density of the tiger population, and so on.

The American expert Chuck McDougal, in his excellent book *The Face of the Tiger*, based on his observations in the Royal Chitwan National Park in Nepal, mentions the apparent preponderance of adult females over males in any given area. He bases his figures on those given by old-time shikaris, and quotes the experiences of himself and Schaller in their respective study areas, where tigresses did appear to outnumber tigers. Taking into account the fact that the sexes of unborn foetuses found in tigresses shot in the wild are equally divided, and also that the figures of births in captivity are equally balanced, he came to the conclusion that some process of attrition must thin out wild males before they reach maturity.

In my experience, however, the difference is more apparent than real; I believe it is an illusion, caused by the fact that males are both more independent and more strongly territorial than females. Since the range of one dominant tiger encompasses those of several females, there is always a number of nomadic young males waiting in the wings for a chance to take over permanently when the present incumbent retires.

According to zoo data, a tigress may first come into season when she is two and a half, and copulation may take place then, but conception is not normally possible until the age of four. (One female at Whipsnade Zoo is said to have had cubs at the age of two, but even if she did, it was a freak.) In the wild, with the stress of solitary living and the constant search for food, natural processes are still further retarded, and four to five seems to be the normal age for a first litter. Though tigresses breed at any season of the year, the chief times are November to January and May and June. The three matings which I have been fortunate enough to monitor all took place in these last two months.

Mating sessions are intense, long-drawn-out affairs, usually lasting three days and three nights, during which period the couple remain in one small area, without breaking off to hunt. Gestation in zoos has been found to average 105 days, and the number of cubs born varies from one to five; although eight foetuses have been reported. Two or three cubs is probably the most usual number. The size of families is controlled mainly, I believe, by habitat conditions and the amount of prey available. If the habitat becomes degraded, and conditions are crowded or harsh, the number of cubs falls in a natural form of population control. Over all, it is estimated that usually only one cub from each litter survives to maturity.

If all goes well, the relationship between a tigress and her cubs is by far the longest and most stable of any association in tiger society, for the young remain with their mother until they are two years old, and during that time she does not come into season again. If, on the other hand, the cubs are killed prematurely, she may re-start her cycle within a period of four to eight months and mate again, to repair the loss. It is this natural mechanism that has led many writers to suggest that a male tiger kills his own cubs if he gets the chance, thus instinctively hastening his next opportunity of contributing his genes to posterity. (My own observations have convinced me that this is quite untrue, although it is possible that a male will kill cubs other than his own.)

Young cubs are extremely affectionate towards their mother, and will rub themselves against her on all occasions, especially when they have been separated from her, even for a brief time. They are also very playful, and like other higher mammals have a distinct sense of fun, jumping repeatedly off tree-branches into water. I saw exactly the same trait in Prince, the male leopard I reared, who loved climbing to the top of a thin tree by a river, knowing that it would bend under his weight and deposit him in the water. (Schaller recently observed a giant panda in the wild repeatedly climbing a snow-slope and tobogganing down it on his backside.)

The tigress, in return, is extremely solicitous of her young – far more so than the social lion. A mother with small cubs is liable to be aggressive towards other tigers and humans, and many people have been threatened or actually attacked by a tigress protecting her family. Normally the defence merely takes the form of a demonstration, but it may develop into an attack, especially if the person being threatened runs away. In the Chitwan National Park, Kirti Man Tamang, a scientist working for the Smithsonian Institution on a radio telemetry programme, was dragged down out of a tree by a tigress with three cubs, getting severely mauled and bitten.

Only when guarding a family does a normal tigress go for humans in this way. Usually both males and females are extremely retiring and do their best to keep out of the way. Even when surprised in a sudden confrontation with a human being, they almost always vanish silently into the nearest undergrowth. If one walks through the jungle in the daytime, one hardly ever sees them. They are there, lying up in the cool of thickets or tall grass, waiting for the fall of night; but the clumsy human, his senses atrophied by so-called civilisation, usually blunders past without spotting them.

A great deal of information about tigers' movements and behaviour can be gleaned from a study of their pug-marks – although tracking is not so exact a science as some people have claimed. It has been suggested that each big cat's pug-marks are as distinctive as the fingerprints of a human being, but this is not so: the texture of the ground varies so much – from rock through gravel to sand, hard earth, soft earth and mud – that tracking cannot be equated with fingerprinting, and long experience is needed to interpret whatever marks the tiger has made.

Nevertheless, it is possible to distinguish the pugs of a male, which are squarer and have thicker toes, from those of a female, with their narrower pads and slimmer toes. Other indicators are the length of stride and the relative placement of front and back feet. Seamed and cracked pads, with spread-out toes, indicate old age, and an idea of weight and size can be gained from the depth of indentation in soft ground.

Unless one of the pugs has some abnormality or deformity, it is not normally possible to distinguish between different animals of the same sex and size. Similarly, it is hard to tell the pugs of a young tiger from those of a full-grown leopard – although experience teaches that a tiger cub's toes are thicker in relation to its pad than those of a leopard. Only people constantly in touch with these animals are able to spot such differences accurately – and even they can slip up on occasions.

It is thus both futile and misleading to claim – as recent census-takers have done – that one tiger can be told from another by his pugs as surely as one human being can from another by his fingerprints. Such claims, founded on ignorance, have led to greatly exaggerated estimates of population increases.

Many more facets of tiger behaviour will, I hope, emerge in the course of the narrative that follows. But perhaps enough has been said here to give some idea of how these marvellous animals organise their lives.

6

THE LEOPARDS

My own close association with the Great Cats began – fortuit-
ously – just as the international movement to save the tiger was
gathering steam. In the summer of 1971 I was offered an
orphaned leopard cub, which had been reared in Calcutta to the
age of three months by Anne Wright, a leading conservationist.
By this time the animal had become altogether too big and
obstreperous for life in a city, and, together with her daughter
Belinda, Anne brought him to Lucknow, where I met the party
with a Jeep and drove them the rest of the way to Tiger Haven.

In due course I called the leopard Prince, and as I have already
told his story in my book *Prince of Cats*, I will recall here only the
highlights of his upbringing. My aim from the start was to see if
it would be possible to return a hand-reared carnivore to the
wild. I therefore gave Prince complete freedom and used few
restraints. I disciplined him as little as possible, for I wanted his
instincts to assert themselves as naturally as they could.

My main problem at first was to overcome his fear of the
forest. Whether or not this was the product of his urban infancy,
I do not know, but to start with he seemed thoroughly scared of
the dense, green world of the jungle, and it was only by taking
him for daily walks that I gradually got him used to it.

75

In the early days he lived in and around the house. Later, to encourage him to spend more time in the jungle, I built him various machans, the biggest and most successful of which I called Leopard Haven, about a mile west of the farm. Gradually, with help and encouragement from me, he learnt to hunt and open up his kills, and became able to feed himself. Finally, in May 1973, when he was just under two years old, he left Tiger Haven to establish himself in the jungle as a fully wild leopard.

My association with him taught me an enormous amount, not least that leopards are by no means the treacherous, unpredictable creatures that people take them for. Prince's character was in many ways more attractive than that of humans. Not only did he show me the warmest affection, rubbing himself against my legs like a domestic cat and sitting pressed up against me as we relaxed by the river: he also demonstrated time and again that he was incapable of harbouring resentment. This was never more clearly shown than on the night when he attacked a buffalo calf in a shed a short distance from the house: to make him release the animal, two of us started beating him with cane stalks, whereupon he let go and disappeared into the darkness. Had he been human, I should certainly have expected a counter-attack. Instead, he quickly materialised out of the night rubbing himself against me in the friendliest possible way.

One of the most remarkable features of his upbringing was his association with Eelie, my little mongrel bitch, who had come to me as a woebegone stray. It is common knowledge that dogs are a favourite item on a wild leopard's menu; but, far from trying to eat Eelie, Prince struck up an extraordinary friendship with her, playing for hours, accompanying her on walks, and investigating the secrets of the forest in her company. Admittedly she was – and is – an exceptionally strong character, able to dominate not only a leopard, but also an elephant and a tiger. Yet in his partnership with her Prince showed both forbearance and high intelligence. Even when he became three times her size, he took great care not to hurt her while playing; he knew her not as a dog but as an individual.

For me, it was intensely rewarding to have shared in the existence of a wild animal, and to see how, as he approached maturity, his wild instincts asserted themselves. In his adolescence he had depended heavily on me for food and security; but then, as he grew up, the call of his own kind proved more powerful than anything I had been able to offer him. Once he had severed the bond between us, he never attempted to re-establish it: although I have several times seen him since, and although he has frequently revisited Tiger Haven during his nocturnal travels, he has gone completely wild.

One tragedy marred the success of my experiment. While I was away on a rare trip to Delhi, Prince mauled the eight-year-old son of my elephant-keeper, and as the result of poor care in hospital, the boy later died. His father had been expressly forbidden to bring him to the farm, but this fact did nothing to damp down local resentment, and the animosity which the incident engendered led indirectly to other disasters later on.

Once Prince was well launched, I became anxious to furnish him with a mate, and by a great stroke of luck in the autumn of 1973 I was presented with two female cubs by no less a person than the Prime Minister, Mrs Indira Gandhi. I named them Harriet and Juliette, and brought them up at Tiger Haven exactly as I had brought up Prince.

Juliette, alas, did not survive into maturity. One day in April 1974, when I was away from home, my men found her lying dead in shallow water at the edge of the river. An unsatisfactory post-mortem did not immediately reveal any cause of death, but I discovered later, from the expert examination of samples taken from her viscera, that traces of alkaloid poison were present, and there seemed no doubt that someone from the Forest Department had murdered her, for she had taken to putting in ill-judged appearances at the Park Headquarters, and the staff there were scared of her.

Harriet at least lived long enough to mate with Prince (who returned to the area of Tiger Haven for a series of courtships) and to produce two families by him. The first, of two cubs, was born on a machan which I had built specially for the event. The mother moved them to a den of her own choosing in the forest, and then, when the monsoon floods rose, decided of her own accord to bring them to the place that offered her the greatest security – Tiger Haven. To entertain a she-leopard and her cubs, at her invitation, was intensely moving: the family lived with us for ten days in one of the spare bedrooms before instinct told Harriet to move them back to the jungle.

She returned to the forest, demanding, in characteristic fashion, to be rowed across the river by me on two successive journeys, while on each trip she carried one cub in her mouth. Then, after only a fortnight in the jungle, the family was threatened more and more closely by the animal I knew as the Big Tigress, whose own cubs had just been trampled to death by a herd of disorientated elephants. Goaded by the loss, driven on by her unfulfilled mother instinct, she called continuously for days and nights on end. Searching compulsively for her own cubs, she found the baby leopards, killed one of them, and forced Harriet to drown the other inadvertently as, in her alarm, she tried to bring it to the safety of the farm.

Harriet's second pregnancy produced only one female cub, which I named Mameena, after Rider Haggard's Child of Storm. For nearly a year I had the great privilege of watching mother and daughter go about their business, partly round Tiger Haven, partly deeper in the jungle. Then, in 1978, came double disaster: in May Mameena was run over by a train, and in November Harriet was found dead scarcely a hundred yards from the farm buildings. Whether or not she had been poisoned, or bitten by a snake, I shall never be sure, for her body was much decomposed by the time we discovered it. Whatever the truth, her loss was a bitter blow to me.

To have known these magnificent cats, and to have shared their lives, was in itself a wonderful experience. I found in the leopards a strong capacity for affection, and an essential tranquillity of temperament, far removed from the meanness and unpredictability so often ascribed to their kind. As I wrote in *Prince of Cats*, I saw that their behaviour was dictated 'by the very basics of existence – the need to kill and avoid being killed', and that they were 'blessedly free from such wretched human characteristics as greed, resentment and malice'.

The loss of Harriet was a great tragedy. On the other hand, I had by then become deeply involved in another project, with still more far-reaching consequences: the hand-rearing and reintroduction to the jungle of the tigress whom I called Tara.

7

OLD CROOKED FOOT

Although I became temporarily preoccupied with the leopards, I had not ceased to be interested in wild tigers. Far from it: I was keenly aware of their activities in the neighbourhood – and so were the leopards, Prince in particular showing an instinctive dread whenever he scented traces of the senior predator.

In the early 1970s the Tiger Haven range was held by the male whom I came to know as Old Crooked Foot, although when I first saw him he did not have the deformity which later gave him his name. My first glimpse of him had come in 1969, when he was still young. One morning in May I was sitting on a well-screened machan above Prince's Pool, a shallow depression in a bend of the Neora river which fills with flood water every year during the monsoon, and then gradually dries out. Jamun trees crowd round it, leaning inwards, and the pool offers not only a favourite drinking-place for the local wild animals, but also a mud wallow much used by sambar and pigs. Many wading birds also fish in the shallow water.

My aim that morning was to film sambar, and I settled down to wait for some to arrive. For a while the jungle was quiet; then my thoughts were interrupted by the appearance of a large black pig, who emerged from the grass to the north, dug his snout into the liquid ooze, and ploughed through it for some distance in the manner of his kind before rolling luxuriously on to his back.

Suddenly a peahen squawked, and flew up in alarm from some bushes to the west. The pig vanished as if by magic. A moment later a tiger appeared, walking towards the pond. Unfortunately he heard the whirr of my cine-camera, changed direction, and moved slowly away under an interlaced roof of greenery, pausing to squirt his scent on to an angled branch before disappearing into a patch of grass.

This was the young tiger on whom the mantle of resident male had descended by default, his predecessor having been shot. Had anyone told me then that he would occupy the range for the next eight years, I should have thought the remark absurdly optimistic, for in those dark days *no* tiger seemed to have much chance of living that long. In fact, by a combination of his own good sense and a change of heart on the part of humans, he survived.

I did not see him again until the following spring. For a while in early 1970 we heard no alarm calls in the vicinity of Tiger Haven, and the winter nights were silent except for the plaintive calls of the fish eagles and the occasional wail of a roosting peacock. I tied out a bait regularly on the site opposite the Double-Storey Machan, but for night after night it remained unvisited, so I tried shifting it further to the west. There, a few nights later, it was killed by a tiger.

Since I knew that in the winter months tigers generally spend the day lying up in the forest, rather than in grass, because they find the jungle warmer, I reckoned that the tiger would have to cross the river to return to his kill; so I had a machan put up in a tree that would command his approach. Hardly had I settled on the platform when I had the great satisfaction of seeing the tiger, whom I recognised as the one from Prince's Pool, come over the river in a spectacular cat-walk along the trunk of a tree that had fallen across the stream. Already he had put on bulk, and as I watched him intermittently over the next six years I saw him grow into a truly magnificent cat, some ten feet long, weighing perhaps 500 lbs, with a shortish tail, indistinct

Right *Harriet the she-leopard at Tiger Haven*

Arjan Singh with Juliette (left) *and Harriet*

below left Eelie playing with Harriet

right Tara arrives at Tiger Haven

below Eelie and Tara playing by river

shoulder stripes, and the large white eye-patches which seem to be a speciality of our local breed.

In the hot days of summer I used to stalk him as he sat in the water. Like all his kind, as he grew in age and self-confidence he spent more and more hours cooling himself: once he had a kill, he would stay in the river the whole day, and at night he would sometimes feed there as well, for he took kills into the water, confident in the knowledge that immersion would preserve them from flies and maggots – although of course he then had other scavengers to contend with, in the form of turtles and the occasional crocodile.

Sometimes I came on him unawares – as on one memorable day when I was bicycling down the Am Danda (literally the 'Mango Road'). As I passed some logs of timber lying on the forest floor, I heard a movement, and thought it odd that the sawyers had arrived for work so early in the morning. Then, sticking out from behind a bush, I saw the head of the tiger, who was scratching his cheek against the shrubbery. His eyes were closed in an ecstatic expression of tigerish bliss, and it was not until I had ridden past within six feet of him that he suddenly heard me and lumbered off into the forest. So close had I been to him that later, when I analysed the encounter, I realised that what had made the greatest impact on my sub-conscious mind was the dimensions of his outsize testicles!

By then I had found that the range immediately surrounding the farm was generally patrolled by two male tigers with overlapping territories. The reason they were prepared to share each other's ground to some extent may have been the abun-dance of prey-chital and swamp deer. Perhaps the fact that I was putting out baits also encouraged them. Unfortunately the Number Two male – a fine, rangy animal – was shot by a local farmer when he strayed outside the sanctuary. (This particular killer was satisfied with the mere act of murder, and did not even take the trouble to preserve the skin. Needless to say, it was a long time before I could bring myself to speak to him again.)

This left the resident male with undisputed mastery of both

Above *An evening stroll: Tara, Eelie and Harriet*
Below *Tara spraying a tree trunk*

territories. In the summer of 1975 he disappeared when the monsoon broke, moving up, as always, on to the higher ground of the escarpment, to keep away from the floods. When the waters began to subside at the end of September I expected to see him any day, for in earlier years he had always made a round of the baiting sites soon after his return. (Such visits, after four months' absence, undoubtedly establish that the large cats have a primitive form of memory.) That autumn, however, he did not reappear until late in December, and when he did come, his pug-marks showed that his right fore-paw was twisted sharply outwards. Now the obvious name for him was Old Crooked Foot.

The cause of the deformity was not immediately apparent, but it seemed clear that he had sustained some injury, for although advancing years are liable to distort a tiger's pads, this crookedness was too marked, and had come on too suddenly, to have been caused by old age alone. Another fact which pointed to an injury was his increased dependence on baits, and he was hungry enough to make regular visits to a kill-site above which I had installed a light, operated from across the river by a dimmerstat, or regulator, so that it could be turned on and off very slowly. Although I saw him several times, I was unable to determine what it was that had twisted his foot: he had no limp, and from a distance he looked intact. Enlightment did not come until later.

The next three months passed uneventfully, and in March I heard him mating with the female known to us as the Big Tigress. Later he returned to his favourite baiting site opposite the Haldu Machan, and to give us more chance of seeing him I put up a series of simple tree-platforms on the route between the kill-site and the grass in which he would often lie up for the day. The best viewing-place was a broad stretch of short grass, across which he approached the kill.

One day we happened to have as house-guests a naval lieutenant-commander and his wife from the American Embassy in New Delhi, Sid and Jackie Sommers, and to give them the best possible opportunity of seeing the Tiger I installed them on a machan built into a shisham tree, over-looking the short grass. The tree had blown over in a storm, but branches had continued to grow vertically from the leaning trunk, and the machan was tied into some forks about ten feet off the ground. The platform was in the open, so that the outlines of people sitting on it were clearly visible.

When the tiger came out of the grass from the west, on his way to the kill, a slight west wind was blowing, so that he did not at first smell anything amiss, even though he passed within twenty yards of the tree, and the occupants of the machan were overflowing the sides of the small platform in their eagerness to take photographs. Even though the tree stuck up out of a bare plain, the tiger walked past unaware of their presence – until suddenly the appalling stench of people – and white people at that – assailed his nostrils.

With a volley of coughing roars he whipped round and charged the tree. At the foot of it he sat down, roaring, growling and champing his jaws. Sid afterwards told me that his hands froze so completely that he was unable to go on taking pictures: both he and Jackie thought their last moments had come. They were not to know that this was only a mock charge, designed to show displeasure. So great was the volume of sound that Harriet heard it a mile away as she was being brought home on a leash for her dinner: as the roars carried through the jungle she shot up a tree, leash and all, urinating freely from on high, and it was not until her keeper finally climbed up to her an hour later that she could be persuaded to come down. Meanwhile Old Crooked Foot, after spending some time glaring malevolently at the Americans, had stalked off back to the grass patch, jerking his tail up and down in a gesture of protest.

It was a thousand pities that Sid gave up filming prematurely, as he had the opportunity of a lifetime. Even so, one of his transparencies, developed later, did reveal the cause of Old Crooked Foot's deformity: the film showed a long scar on his shoulder, and although I could not be certain, it seemed likely that this was the remains of a gunshot wound. The injury, along with advancing age, no doubt contributed to the uncertainty of his temper, which we witnessed several times more.

In May 1976 Dieter Plage, the distinguished cameraman from Anglia Television, came to the park to make a film about tigers (now, as I write, it is estimated that the film has been seen by 250 million people in ninety-six countries). Another bait was taken, and Old Crooked Foot obligingly mounted a second demonstration by charging another machan. Again, it was a display of distaste, rather than a real attack, but it confirmed to me once again that tigers have a very keen sense of smell, which they use frequently, but which they do not depend on entirely, as their sight and hearing are equally acute. Furthermore, I really do believe that what excited his hostility was the smell of foreigners, for local tigers, living in close proximity to people, are smelling Indians all the time, and derive more useful information from scents and sounds than we give them credit for.

Although Anglia Television unfortunately did not manage to film Old Crooked Foot when he charged the machan, they got plenty of footage out of him. Not only was he a large tiger: he was also partly diurnal in his habits. After the first rains, in June, the camera team got some lively sequences of him and the Big Tigress swimming in a pool of water; later, we sat and filmed him in the river from early afternoon until nearly sunset. Unlike younger tigers, he did not bother to come out every now and then to dry himself in the breeze, but sat immersed in the stream, occasionally flicking his tail and changing position when he lowered his great head to drink, and watching with idle interest as clusters of leaves floated by. Once, as we observed him through a 1,000mm lens, we saw a series of bubbles rise from under his tail, and the frown on his brow as he surveyed these gaseous eruptions seemed to indicate that he was wondering where they came from!

It was not long before we had another formidable display of his temper. One night at the Dimmerstat Machan I watched the Big Tigress feeding on a bait that he had killed earlier, but she seemed particularly watchful and ill-at-ease. Then suddenly she glanced behind her and left in a hurry. I walked home, but soon afterwards we heard the noise of elephants crossing the Neora near the Leopard Flyover: the crashing and snapping of branches, and occasional squeals from the young ones, told us that part of the herd was heading towards the kill. All at once harsh roars began to tear through the darkness as Old Crooked Foot vented his rage against the intruders. The elephants trumpeted and fled to the west, and in the morning we saw from the tracks where they had been confronted by the single, irate old gentleman, whose volatile temper had enabled him to see them off.

Altogether the elephants were in a dangerously aggressive frame of mind: in recent weeks they had overturned a tractor, smashed signposts at railway crossings, raided crops, held up motor traffic in a rampage of knocking down trees (which they did not bother to eat), and surrounded and trampled to death a female sambar. I could not blame them for their aggression, however, as I knew the cause of it: they had been driven out of their ancestral habitat in Nepal by heavy timber-felling, and had reached Dudhwa in a thoroughly truculent mood. (Later, when they settled down and got to know the area, they reverted to their normal placid state.)

Old Crooked Foot faded from our scene at the end of 1977, and his range was taken over by younger animals. He had been an exceptionally intolerant tiger – probably due to his wound – and in the later years of his regime he had allowed no other male to operate on his ground. With advancing years and the pressure of his slight disability he acquired extraordinary boldness, which drove him to pull a buffalo out of a yoked cart on no fewer than four occasions. Once as a string of seven carts was creaking and squeaking along the metalled road from the Nepal border, he attacked the second team in line. In spite of the shouts of the cartmen, he dragged the buffalo off into the forest and killed it: such was his strength.

This kind of outrageous behaviour ceased with his disappearance, and the fact that nothing similar has happened since suggests that only a tiger of exceptional power and confidence would make such brazen attacks.

His final exit from the range remains something of a mystery, but I believe he died of old age and wounds after a fight with an adversary. Tigers do die of old age and as the result of battles with rivals – a natural process which eliminates the aged and the halt. Their mortal remains are rarely found, for their bodies are quickly eroded and buried in the humus that enriches the soil.

Several times in 1978 wildlife guards at Bhadraula spotted an ancient tiger who walked hesitantly and whose skin hung in folds. Conscious of his waning powers, and with his confidence sapped by age, Old Crooked Foot had moved out of his former haunts to become a nomad and eke out his final years on fringe pickings. No longer would we hear his proud call clearing the way of lesser intruders: from now on he would always be a trespasser, evicted or tolerated by younger tigers into whose range he had wandered. Old age comes to the great cats with a terrifying finality.

After those few appearances at Bhadraula, he was seen no more, and some time later his remains were found in a stand of grass. All round where he lay, patches of cover had been flattened in a death struggle, which had ranged over a wide area. His skull, which was intact, had the molars considerably worn; one incisor was missing, and the rest were almost level with the gums, while the canines, which in his prime would have been full and craggy, were thin and smooth as railroad spikes.

Sad though it was to hear of the death of a former friend, I found comfort in my reflection that his end had not been brought about by any self-styled sport-killer. It is thus that natural selection works, and thus that healthy populations are maintained among wild predators.

8

TARA

In 1975, with Project Tiger in full swing, I conceived the idea of doing my own small part for the rescue scheme by seeing if it would be possible to bring up a hand-reared tiger and return it to the jungle, as I had returned Prince. Harriet was then still alive, and I hoped that in due course she too would make a full return to the wild, but meanwhile I became eager to try my hand with a tiger as well.

Local politics and bureaucratic obstruction made it impossible to mount such a scheme without overriding authority from the Central Government, and I therefore wrote direct to Mrs Gandhi, who had demonstrated her concern for wildlife so practically by presenting me with the pair of leopard cubs. Her reaction was splendid: a letter from the Prime Minister's secretariat said that she approved of my tiger project, and that a search was being mounted for suitable cubs.

It seemed too good to be true – and so it was. For various reasons no cubs could be found, and the one which I eventually obtained came to me through the agency of Dieter Plage, the Anglia Television cameraman. It was as a result of his interest and help that, in 1976, we located a suitable cub at Twycross Zoo, in England.

In July that year I flew from Delhi to London and proceeded at once to Twycross, where I met the zoo's owner, Molly Badham, and the keeper who had hand-reared the female cub until then, John Voce. The tigress was then three months old, and the first snag was that although she knew John well, she did not know me at all, and her initial reaction to me was hostile.

To get to know her, and enable her to get to know me, I spent the next few days in her company, either in her cage or just outside it, in the passage. Although I collected quite a few bites, and had one pair of trousers torn to shreds, I felt confident that my continual presence would soon erode her suspicion and hostility. So it proved: on the third day she rubbed herself against the wire netting, on which I was leaning from the other side, and treated me to a *Prusten*.

By the fourth day I felt that we knew each other well enough to travel together, and we would have set out at once on our 6,000-mile journey, had it not been for a sinister telephone call from Delhi, where some wildlife official suddenly announced that since none of the Bengal tigers bred in European zoos was of pure Indian descent, I was in no circumstances to import one of them to the sub-continent. To release a 'genetic cocktail' into the jungle, the man said, would have a disastrous effect on the purity of the sub-species.

To me, this was scientific nonsense, but luckily the need to argue was temporarily removed by the fact that Dr Bernhard Grzimek – Head of the Frankfurt Zoo and a leading light in European conservation circles – endorsed my project, and offered to present the cub to Mrs Gandhi as a gift symbolising his personal support for Project Tiger. Thus fortified, I ignored the call from Delhi and set out for home.

From Twycross, Tara (in a cage) and I travelled by truck to Heathrow Airport. There she was loaded into the baggage hold of a Pan American Boeing 747, and to make sure that the cage did not slide about, we lashed it to one of the struts. I was full of misgivings about what might happen if the flight got rough, but when I went back into the hold during our first stop in Frankfurt, I found Tara in much better spirits than I had expected, and she was calm enough to drink some milk. A new crew, even more considerate than the first, took us on to

Teheran, and thence to Delhi. The thirteen-hour flight had gone far better than I had dared hope.

As if to take their revenge on me for having enjoyed good fortune so far, the Indian Customs launched the kind of delaying action of which only they were capable, and, to cut short an extraordinarily boring story, it was fifteen days before I could obtain clearance to remove Tara from the Delhi Zoo, where she had been temporarily interned. Then at last we were free to set out on the final lap of our journey. Leaving in the early morning to avoid the heat, we drove to my brother Balram's farm at Jasbirnagar, some ten miles short of Tiger Haven, and then, because the monsoon floods were still high, and the road impassable to vehicles, we completed the journey with the tigress's cage lashed on the back of Sitara, my elephant. It seemed rather appropriate that Tara, having flown by jumbo jet, should arrive at her new home on elephant-back.

Before my trip to England I had already made some preparations for Tara's reception – for instance, wiring-in various verandahs so that I would be able to protect her from the attentions of any wild tiger that might wander past the house. Now the most urgent necessity was to introduce her to Harriet and Eelie.

About Eelie I felt confident: she had worked out relationships with Prince and Harriet so easily that I was sure she would do the same with Tara – and so it proved. After cautious introductions by me, lasting three days, the little bitch established her dominance over the tiger cub with a few well-placed nips, and from that moment they got on perfectly.

Harriet was another matter. As she had lost her own cubs to a tigress, I feared that she might react aggressively against one of her natural enemies. Sure enough: the first time she returned to Tiger Haven after a spell in the jungle, she was exceedingly nervous, and even though she could not *see* Tara inside her temporary cage, she obviously sensed a hostile presence and rushed up a tree, from which she came down only to go back across the river into the forest. Not until ten days had passed did I consider it safe to let her and Tara meet in the open. There were a few tense moments as each tested the other's reactions, but after a couple of scuffles I could see that everything was going to work out, and the two gradually settled down to a working relationship.

When I began taking both Tara and Harriet for walks, we presented a curious sight: a man, a dog, a full-grown leopard and a small tiger in procession along the jungle paths. Every now and then Tara would take a playful rush at Harriet, but if the leopard happened to look round and see her coming, she would either suddenly desist from her attempt at ambush, or convert the attack into one on Eelie – exactly what I had seen Harriet and her sister do when *they* were cubs. Harriet, for her part, seemed to look on the young tigress as a substitute cub, and became quite possessive about her.

Like Prince, Tara was at first scared of the jungle and reluctant to enter it, but gradually our walks increased her confidence. My aim was to help her establish a range, and so let the resident tigers know that a newcomer had arrived in their area. Potentially the most formidable competitor was the Big Tigress who had killed Harriet's cubs: I knew she was still around, for I had heard her mating, and there was a strong possibility that she might attack Tara – a stranger – especially if she came on her without warning.

For a few weeks we were confined to the southern bank of the river by the monsoon floods, but after that we were able to extend our excursions into the forest to the north. Tara grew with amazing speed. By the end of the year she was bigger than Harriet in every way – both longer and thicker – and she made Eelie look like a toy dog, for at six months old she weighed at least 150 lbs. With me and anyone else she knew she was always most affectionate, but she did not like strange humans, who made her palpably nervous. It was fascinating to see how accurately she recognised individuals, be they human, canine or feline. There was no question of her being friendly to all dogs or all leopards: it was just that she knew Eelie and Harriet as individuals, and got on with them.

One difficulty, as she grew larger, was that her affection for me often took the form of boisterousness. Often she jumped on me, and sometimes she would stand on her hind legs boxing at me with her front paws. So by the end of the year a fair number of my clothes were in tatters, and I had sustained a good many bites and scratches. She never intended the slightest harm, but her sheer size and weight became a problem. The reason she took such liberties with me was that I never tried to discipline her: I hardly ever hit her back or tried to knock her down. My easy-going approach sprang not from soft-heartedness, but rather from a deliberate policy of trying not to imprint the tigress with human discipline or inhibit her natural reactions, for I knew that once she grew up her success in hunting and avoiding other tigers would depend on the speed of her reflexes, and I was afraid that if these were dulled or slowed by memories of being punished, the effect might be disastrous.

As a cub, her main method of communicating with me was a high-pitched *ah-ah*, but as she grew up she began to use *Prusten*, blowing out through closed lips, and I would respond in kind. When looking for her in the jungle or round the farm, I would call her by her name.

Already, with Prince and Harriet, I had realised that there was not much I could teach budding predators, except to help them become familiar with the jungle. All the same, it was fascinating to watch Tara's deep-rooted instincts start to develop and assert themselves. On New Year's Day, 1977, she sprayed for the first time – a sure sign that she was growing up. Not long after that she made her first kill: a chital fawn which got caught up in creepers when the rest of its herd ran away. Even so, her hunting ability was still amateurish. If we found a single animal, and I went with her when she began to stalk it, the odds were that she would suddenly lose interest in the real quarry and jump on me instead. One day I let her out of the cage built on to the back of a Jeep in full view of a herd of swamp deer, and although she began to stalk them with a fair degree of skill, she soon gave up her patient approach in favour of an all-out chase, which of course produced chaos, as 200 or more animals took off through the tall grass in every conceivable direction. Tara seemed to enjoy it, and so did the deer, for they charged round in circles instead of making good their escape – but of course she caught nothing.

In March 1977, when she was ten months old, there occurred an event of which she could have no inkling, but which threatened her future in an unpleasant fashion. At the general election the population rounded on Mrs Gandhi, their former idol, threw out her Congress Party, and elected instead a number of smaller opposition groups which united to form the Janata Party. Grassroots democracy was now all the cry, and immediately I became anxious about the future of wildlife – always an early casualty in times of political unrest.

In my own district things certainly looked unpropitious, for local forestry contractors began to demand that commercial forestry should be re-started in the Dudhwa Park, and I realised belatedly that although Mrs Gandhi had backed my tiger project (and indeed had officially given Tara to me) the experiment had never been formally sanctioned by the State authorities, who might well now turn against it. Even without an official pronouncement local people wrote to their Member of Parliament demanding that Tara be kept away from all inhabited areas, on the grounds that she was a potential man-eater, because she had been brought up by humans and therefore had no fear of them.

I did what I could to allay animosity by going to see the Forest Department official in charge of wildlife, and also our local Member of Parliament, both of whom I knew. Apart from that, my best course seemed to be to press ahead with Tara's education as fast as possible and trust that she would keep out of harm's way.

The need for vigilance was emphasised in the middle of April, just before her first birthday, when my filwan, or elephant-keeper, told me that he had seen the Big Tigress sitting outside the same patch of ratwa grass two days running. This, together with a reckoning of dates, made me certain that she once again had a family of cubs. Assuming that she was liable to be more aggressive than usual, I tried to keep her away from the area which Tara and I were frequenting by feeding her some baits. This worked for a while – but then came the inevitable clash.

By then the weather had grown hot, and even though Tara had a water-tank inside her day-cage, she soon found she preferred to spend the afternoons in the river, at a point some fifty yards upstream from the house. One afternoon two loud defensive roars burst out suddenly from beyond the Junction

Bridge. I rushed outside with a shout and saw Tara galloping towards the bridge with the Big Tigress close after her. Tara came up the bank, but her pursuer spun round and bolted the moment she saw me. As I was chasing her off, Tara disappeared, but when I called her she came out of the undergrowth and twice sprayed the bridge in a release of tension. Although she was unhurt, it had been a narrow escape, and for the next day or two she was rather subdued. The incident made me anxious, for, with cubs to protect, the Big Tigress would remain a potential danger for several months.

The best I could do was to keep taking Tara for walks and thus increase her knowledge of the range into which I had arbitrarily set her down. Her territory was an area of between fifteen and twenty square miles, bounded on the east by the metalled road running up from Pallia to Dudhwa, and in the north by the road from Dudhwa to Gauriphanta. The western boundary was the fireline cut from the main road past Tiger Well to Chorgatia (literally 'Thieves' Crossing'), and in the south our limit was the ragged frontier of the forest land, where the lush grasses (often fifteen or twenty feet high) gave way to sugar-cane and other cultivated fields.

The approximate centre of the range was the Spillway baiting site, about half a mile west of Tiger Haven, and the river was the scene of much tiger activity, both our own and that of the wild population, especially during the hot weather. To me the river is always a lovely sight: the jungle presses in on either bank, and from the stream there rise the wrecks of many an ancient tree, torn out by monsoon floods and now come to rest in extraordinary attitudes. Bleached by sun and water, and half-buried in the silt-deposits of many years, their grotesque shapes stick up like the ribs of sunken battleships; and among this debris of battered roots, rising Medusa-like from the placid waters, the tigers sit and cool themselves in the heat of the day.

Tara loved the river as much as I did. She would chase Eelie in and out of the shallows, and when the little bitch grew tired she would transfer her attention to me, determined to involve me in her aquatic sports. More than once, as she launched a tremendous spring out of the water, I was knocked flat on to the sand and made forcibly aware of how fast she was putting on bulk. As the monsoon approached, with its usual harbingers of fierce, hot wind-storms, the river became more and more the focus of our peregrinations.

The rains broke late, on June 30, but when they came they were exceptionally violent. Soon not only the grasslands but also the approaches to Tiger Haven were flooded with muddy water; and just as the wild tigers sought refuge on the high ground, so we too were obliged to cross the swollen river and take our walks on top of the escarpment.

For humans, the only means of crossing the torrent was by boat, and we were not helped in our voyages by Tara's nautical experiments. Instead of embarking when we suggested it, she would wait until Babu Lal (her keeper) and I had both climbed in, and then come flying aboard with a great leap that threatened to capsize us all. Finally we had to coax Eelie on board as well; but whereas she had the sense to sit tight in the middle of the slender vessel, Tara would parade up and down, pausing to lean her bulk against the leading oarsman. The only way we could make progress was for one of us to row and the other to devote himself to resisting Tara's great sideways pressure. We would scarcely reach the far bank before the tigress would launch herself off on to the bank and race up the face of the escarpment. In fact she need not have accompanied us in the boat at all, for she was quite capable of swimming the river even when it was in spate, and often did so, with her tail stuck our rigidly behind her, sometimes clear of the water.

The bigger she grew, the more difficult it became to weigh her, but I did get a fairly accurate reading in June, when she turned the balance at just over 200 lbs. By then, whenever she charged me, her paws made a loud and distinctive thudding, and I began to wonder if the noise had some function in intimidating prey species and freezing their flight-reflex during the final seconds of a charge.

At the end of June I observed a fascinating change in the relationship between Tara and Harriet. The leopard, who by then was heavily pregnant, returned to the farm after spending ten days in the jungle, and at once became most aggressive towards the tigress, even though she was by far the smaller of the two. Tara, for her part, grew nervous, and avoided Harriet as much as possible. Even after a single cub had been born on July 1 she continued to efface herself. Once the cub had been weaned, her attitude suddenly changed again, and the two cats again became the best of companions, spending much time together. I was amazed at the subtlety of communication which existed between them.

Throughout the monsoon the Big Tigress continued to harass us with her menacing presence. Tracks showed that she had a single cub, and it was clearly her urge to protect it which made her so aggressive. No one became more closely aware of her displeasure than Babu Lal, who, one day when I was away, took Tara and Eelie for their morning walk along the top of the escarpment towards Dudhwa. On the way back he looked round, to see the Big Tigress following them, and although she slipped into the bushes when he yelled, she reappeared a moment later. Tara became disconcerted, but seemed to recover her composure as she approached home, and went to cool off in the river. Babu Lal sat down on the bank opposite her, with Eelie between them. Suddenly Tara stood up, looked in his direction and gave a nervous *Prusten*. A moment later it occurred to Babu Lal that she was looking not at him but above him, and when he turned he found the Big Tigress standing on the bank not ten yards away. Seeing herself observed, she bounded off – but two days later we again found her following us closely. Her interest in Tara seemed obsessive and (from our point of view) dangerous, so whenever Tara went to sit in the river near Tiger Haven I posted a man with a tin can to raise the welkin if trouble looked like starting.

All this time I had been worried about Tara's lack of any real interest in hunting: almost every time I led her into a stalk she would turn the episode into a game. But now an incident with a porcupine seemed to presage better things. One morning she found a porcupine in some grass, and when it tried to cross the river on a sloping tree she seized it in her mouth by the rump and flicked it towards dry land. When I caught up with her she had one paw resting on the rodent, which was still alive, but as I came up she hooked one paw round my leg as if to ask what she should do next. As the animal was obviously injured, I killed it, and we dragged the carcass back to Tiger Haven, where we skinned and disembowelled it, placing the remains in her cage.

That night she devoured every bit of it, and seemed to take an unusually proprietorial attitude towards the kill. When my tracker, Jackson, went up to her cage she snarled at him, which was surprising as she knew him well and it was normally he who fed her at the time.

I welcomed this as a step forward, and indeed her hunting instinct did seem to be slowly awakening. No doubt if I had fed her less it would have developed faster: as it was, she seemed to have little enthusiasm for eating creatures which she killed – among them two monitor lizards, which she suffocated with her paws, and an old langur which she pinched to death with her claws. Gradually her behaviour became more adult. When confronted by a strong smell – whether of rotting fish, of a dead animal, or even of Jackson in the hot weather – she would use the *Flehmen* grimace of interest. Along the trail, as we were walking, she would react much more positively to signs of another tiger, grimacing, drooling and rolling. Nor was she by any means unaware of the menace of the Big Tigress, who seemed to make her more nervous than any other – and with good reason.

One day the Big Tigress gave vent to her aggression by killing a fishing cat, which she had chased along the road. She had no intention of eating it – she left the body lying on the roadside – and clearly performed the murderous act to protect her cub. I was afraid that if she managed to catch Tara she might do the same to her, for the same reason.

One day at the end of August I went to Lucknow for a wildlife meeting, and on my way back I stopped for the night with friends at Sitapur. At five in the morning I suddenly awoke, having dreamt that I could hear Tara roaring in distress, but that her roars were growing fainter, and that although I was running towards the noise I was getting no closer. I put the incident out of my head, collected some meat for Tara in Lakhimpur, and continued towards home. I reached the Nakauhwa bridge site – the furthest that motor transport could go during the monsoon – late in the afternoon.

Right *Long Toes* – *a rare daytime appearance*

I had just loaded the meat on to the elephant when I saw Babu Lal approaching with a crestfallen look, and at once I knew that something bad had happened. Sure enough, he told me that Tara had been hurt in a fight with the Big Tigress. At once I took off in the Jeep to get veterinary assistance from Pallia, and darkness had fallen before, stumbling and splashing through waist-deep water, we eventually reached Tiger Haven.

Apart from minor scratches, Tara had sustained two deep wounds, one on the outside of her right thigh, and the other on the inside near her anus. The outer wound was so deep, and her skin was so loose, that skin and flesh appeared quite unconnected. The vet announced that he would have to give her three separate jabs – sedative, anti-tetanus and antibiotic – so we put a noose with a sliding knot round her neck, and Babu Lal held her head while I tried to block her sight of the vet. The first injection went in safely, but put her on the look-out for the second, and this she greeted with a powerful snarl. How we gave her the antibiotic shot, I am not sure, but the vet stuck to the task magnificently.

Later I learnt that Tara had been lying under a bush when the Big Tigress leapt on her. We found the undergrowth trampled, some hair, and one splintered claw-casing which was cracked and old, and so must have come from the aggressor. Considering that she had been caught in a prone position, from which she could hardly counter-attack, it seemed that Tara had got away lightly, and no doubt had learned not to sleep so soundly. Even so, she was very lame from her injuries, and had to spend more than three weeks in her cage recovering. The wounds left noticeable scars on both the inside and the outside of her thigh. By the beginning of October, when the monsoon had come to an end, Tara was more mature and independent. Now, at seventeen months, she would often branch off during our walks in the forest and return home on her own; she also marked her territory more widely by spraying, but although she showed greater interest in prey animals, she still ran after them, as a dog does, rather than stalking them in true tiger fashion.

Physically, she had become a real handful. Although

Above *Tara at sixteen months*
Below *Old Crooked Foot demonstrates against American intruders*

infinitely careful not to hurt Eelie, who she always avoided in the last few seconds of a charge, she would leap on me with the greatest delight, and I am convinced that some elementary sense of humour made her positively enjoy knocking me down, especially if she could get me into the river. Still anxious not to discipline her, I tried various ways of deflecting her, such as cracking a split bamboo stick at her or banging a tin can: a more effective counter, if I saw her about to charge, was to crouch down and threaten a charge of my own. All this, I hardly need say, was done in fun, and between rough-houses she was as affectionate as ever; but as she now weighed some 250 lbs, she was a force to be reckoned with. For her own protection, I continued to keep her in her cage at night and, even with the lure of a pig-bone, which she could hardly resist, we found it more and more difficult to get her in there.

The middle of November brought a red-letter day, when she made her first kill – or rather when, in an extraordinary combination, she made a kill with the help of Eelie – the first such joint effort by a tiger and a dog, I dare say, that has ever been recorded.

At about three in the afternoon I heard loud distress cries from the patch of grass in which Tara had been spending the day, and as I ran towards them I was overtaken by Eelie, speeding to find out the cause of the disturbance. Arriving on the scene, I saw a sambar fawn standing in the shallow river, where it had taken refuge. Tara had hold of it by one back leg, and was trying to drag it up on to the bank. Quickly I crossed the bridge to get a better view, and what should I see then but the astounding sight of Eelie in charge of the victim: she had driven the tigress off and stood in the water nipping at the fawn. Tara was running up and down the bank in frustration.

Impressed though I was by Eelie's performance, I tied her up, whereupon Tara rushed back into the water and pulled her first kill on to dry land, dragging it up into a copse, where I had the carcass disembowelled for her. The copse was already defended by strips of white cloth, which we had put up to protect Harriet and her cub by frightening off tigers coming from the west, and I hoped they would now serve Tara as well.

On the first evening she ate a good deal from one back leg,

starting at the rump in true tiger fashion, and she spent all next day with the kill, snacking on it from time to time, but greeting me with great affection and exuberance when I went to visit her. By dark, however, news of the kill seemed to have filtered out, in the mysterious way it does, to other potential customers. One tiger called persistently to the south, and later in the night another – the male which I subsequently called Long Toes – came along the north bank of the river and let go a full-throated call right opposite the point at which I was asleep in the open. His tracks showed that he had gone up to the cloth barrier but then turned back, scraping frequently in frustration as he made off. In the morning, Tara finished the carcass herself, and returned to her cage.

Now began the final phase of her association with me. That night another male tiger somehow found his way past the cloth barrier and visited the kill-site. His pug-marks had full pads but relatively short toes, showing that he was a young male, and because of the persistent association that was beginning, I called him Tara's Male. It was undoubtedly his presence on the range which drew her off and accelerated her departure into the wild.

By the end of December she had taken to calling loudly as she came out of her cage in the morning; then, one day, she did not follow me as usual when we set off for our walk, but struck off across the Junction Bridge on her own. Thereafter she kept going off by herself and rolling on spots where the male had rolled in the night.

I could see the break coming. For the moment, however, old loyalties battled with new ones – and never more clearly than one evening in January, when I heard swamp deer calling from near the Haldu Machan and went out to look for her. For a while I called without getting any response, but then she suddenly appeared, came up to me and rubbed her head against my waist, moaning softly. I thought I had noticed her limping, so I looked down at her left forearm and found four slight fang-marks. At that moment a tiger roared in annoyance no more than 200 yards away: obviously she had been with him and he was angry that she had deserted him. It was thrilling to realise that her head, now rubbing against me, must have been in contact with *his* great head a few seconds before.

As the days went by it became more and more difficult to control her movements, as the call of her own kind asserted itself. Every morning an irresistible compulsion drew her into the forest, whence she did not return until dusk or even later. I felt sure she was spending her days with the male.

For some weeks I had been thinking of building an enclosure for her deeper in the jungle, to isolate her more effectively from humans, for I did not want to run any risk that she might become familiar with people as her age and confidence increased. I had therefore applied to the Forest Department for permission, but when it came, after the usual long delay, it authorised me to build not where I had suggested, but in an area that would be completely new to Tara.

To have moved her away from the range which, with my help, she had painstakingly got to know might well have proved disastrous, for she would have arrived as a total stranger in a group of new tigers, any of which might have reacted against her in a hostile way. The scheme was thus a non-starter, and as an alternative I decided to convert Leopard Haven into Tara's headquarters by wiring in the legs of the tree-house to form a large cage in which she could spend her nights. Work began, and I hoped to move her there on January 15. That evening, however, she did not come back to the farm until long after nightfall. We put her food in her inner cage and left a bowl of water near the door, so that if I heard lapping I could quickly close it; then, after waiting up some time, I went to bed. At midnight I heard an animal drinking – not from the bowl, but from the pump a few yards away. I put on the verandah light and advanced towards the noise with a bone in my hand, calling. Presently I saw Tara crouching just below the steps on the verandah, but from her attitude and the look in her eyes I could tell that she was not going to be lured inside, however much she might want the bone. Suddenly she took a dart at me, knocked me against the cage-partition, and dashed out again. I switched off the light and waited until in the end hunger overcame her other priorities and she slipped into the night-cage, whereupon I managed to close the door.

That was the last night she spent at Tiger Haven. When I opened the door of her cage in the morning, she embraced me briefly from the top of the three-foot-high plinth, then did a ritual spray on the pylon in front of the cage and stood around waiting for me to join her in a walk. Harriet and Eelie having also completed their ritual spraying of the pylon, we all set off over the Junction Bridge in the direction of Leopard Haven, where carpenters were putting the finishing touches to Tara's new home.

As we drew near the tree-house I diverted the tigress's attention, for I was afraid that the workmen would be alarmed if they saw her and Harriet approaching. It was at that moment, on the morning of January 16, 1978, that Tara went up the escarpment and chose to sever her connection with human companions. She was twenty months and ten days old.

Since that day, she has never been back. She has stood at the Junction Bridge and called to me. She has sometimes come almost to the house. When I have called to her, she has gazed at me with recognition. But she has never again associated with humans, and she has broken with the past. She now belongs to the world of darkness, those velvet hours between twilight and dawn denied to the human intruder.

The influence of the environment on animal behaviour cannot be over-emphasised. Animals that live out in the open, such as swamp deer and chital, are gregarious and confiding. Those that live in a closed habitat, such as the sambar and barking deer, are withdrawn and shy. The solitary tiger and leopard are both introverted, the social lion – which inhabits open plains – more forthcoming. Whereas Elsa, Joy Adamson's lioness, brought her cubs to her human supporters, both Harriet and Tiffany (my fishing cat) visited me regularly while they had young families, but kept their cubs away. (Harriet, it is true, brought her cubs to Tiger Haven briefly when they were threatened by floods, in a touching display of trust, but moved them back into the forest as soon as she considered the threat was past.)

People have often asked me why, if zoo keepers are recognised by their former charges years after they have left a particular job, neither Prince nor Tara ever came back to me once they had made the initial break. The answer lies in the power of the environment: the switch from a daytime existence, which they shared with humans, to a nocturnal life in the closed circuit and darkness of the deep woods, where they associated only with other animals, erased most of their early memories. The call of their own kind proved so strong that they scarcely recognised their former associate – and indeed, once they had gone, they would not accept any form of dependence. Their new environment had taken them over.

At the time, of course, I could not know that the break would be so final. On the day Tara disappeared I had to go to Delhi, and it was not until later that I learnt from Babu Lal what had happened next. He told me that during the night he had heard a bear grunt and take off in alarm near the Double-Storey Machan. Pug-marks revealed that Tara had come right up to her cage, but not into it; then she had jumped into the boat moored against the bank on the river, and finally swum across. For the next three days she had consorted with Tara's Male – flattened grass in several different places showed where the pair of them had rolled – but she had not been to Tiger Haven any more. She had finally chosen freedom and made her return to the wild.

When I got back to find her still absent, I was greatly surprised, for I had expected her to retain her association with me for many more months, perhaps even until she was old enough to conceive, at the age of three and a half to four. In retrospect, it is clear that what hastened her departure was the presence of the other tigers so close to the farm – but at the time I could not help worrying about her immaturity. Exciting though it was that she had opted for her own kind, as I had always hoped she would, I feared that her limited experience and limited hunting ability might make it impossible for her to survive. I was only too well aware of the fact that I had taught her nothing: there is nothing a human *can* teach wild animals, for his ways are entirely different. All I had done was to allow Tara's deep-seated instincts the best possible chance of asserting themselves, and all I could do now was hope that they would serve her well.

9

TARA'S MALE AND LONG TOES

In the weeks that followed Tara's disappearance, we spent many hours searching for her, and I offered a reward for information about her. Yet all we really discovered was that she was spending much of her time in the company of her male. When we began putting out baits, the manner in which they were despatched showed that tigers more expert than Tara had performed the executions: even if she was feeding on them, she was not actually killing them.

Not long after she had gone I had a clear indication of the way in which tigers can assimilate useful information for their future use. One evening an employee at Tiger Haven climbed on to the roof to discover what had been alarming a group of deer out in front of the buildings, and saw a tiger moving away into the grass beyond the cultivated fields. The animal was too far off for him to recognise it, but, thinking it might be Tara, and being anxious to get a good sighting of her, I walked out in the direction the tiger had taken, calling as I went.

The animal's progress was evident from the nervous cackling of jungle fowl, but I got no answer to my calls, and turned back towards the house. Then, happening to look behind me, I saw that the tiger – Tara's Male – had come back on his tracks, out into the open: as I stood still, he walked to within fifty yards and had a good look at me before moving off. I realised that he associated my voice with Tara's presence, and that, hidden and out of sight, he must often have observed us as we walked along the jungle tracks. To him, my calls were a clear indication that Tara was about.

It was not long before he taught me something else. I tied out another bait, and as the night was a cold one I put a piece of sacking over the buffalo to shield it from the frost. In the morning I found that the bait had not been killed, but tracks showed that Tara's male had come to it sometime during the night. Evidently he had been put off attacking by the unfamiliar appearance of his quarry, for he had sat down to watch his prospective victim from a distance of less than ten yards before moving away. After that he had come on to Tiger Haven, looking for Tara, and then had disappeared up the escarpment. The next night, when I left the sacking off the buffalo, he came and killed it – a perfect example of the way in which the great cats avoid anything unfamiliar.

That same night another tiger appeared on the scene. Though his pads were about the same size as those of Tara's Male, his toes were noticeably longer and thicker, and I had no hesitation in calling him Long Toes. Next morning it was clear that a scuffle had taken place between him and his rival. On a patch of ground which I had ploughed up to help with the identification of pug-marks, an area of about ten square yards had been flattened. Smears of blood and tufts of hair showed that there had been a scrap, and from some deeply-indented tracks I could see that Long Toes had chased Tara's Male across the river and up the escarpment. Both had fed from the kill – as was obvious from the pug-marks round it and from the amount eaten – so it seemed that the dust-up had not been a serious territorial battle.

Burning with curiosity to know exactly what was going on, I decided to spend the next night on the Haldu Machan, opposite the kill. The evening was fine, and I settled on the platform shortly before sundown, at about seven o'clock. Just before nine I heard a tiger feeding and turned on a powerful searchlight. The beam revealed one of the males at his dinner, but I could not tell which it was and quickly switched the lamp off again to avoid disturbing him. Shortly afterwards the stars started to disappear as clouds drifted across the sky, and it was pretty clear that rain was coming. I was determined to stay out as long as I could, and about an hour later, when I turned on the light again, I was rewarded by seeing a different male in action.

Soon after that a few stars peeped through the clouds, but just as I was hoping that the rain might hold off after all, the first drops fell. By midnight the darkness was stygian, and the downpour was such that I felt ready to admit defeat. The snag was that the only way home led past the kill, and I did not much fancy walking by it, especially as I knew about the fight the night before, which had quite likely been the result of a chance encounter.

When I switched on the light for the last time, I was relieved to see there were no tigers on the kill, so I came down and squelched my way past it, through the tenacious clay, furtive and bedraggled in the pelting rain. Wherever the tigers had got to by then, they accorded me a free passage. The relief of reaching a warm bed seemed to make all the discomfort of the excursion worthwhile.

Next morning we found that the kill had been completely eaten out by the two males. Tara had not come to it, and as time passed it became clear that she did not wish to associate with both males at the same time.

My first clear view of Long Toes came on March 24. On my way to Park Headquarters at Dudhwa by Jeep, I saw a tiger sitting on his hunkers outside a patch of narkul reeds near the Croc Bend: he had a large head and scarcely-noticeable eye-patches, which gave him a rather saturnine appearance. When he moved off, I went over and looked at his tracks and realised that this was Long Toes. That evening he took a bait in front of the Narkul Machan, and I saw him again as he came to the kill in the dusk. Two sightings in daylight made it something of a red-letter day – and I had a further bonus in the form of a clear illustration of tiger protocol.

Soon after Long Toes had begun feeding on the kill, Tara's Male appeared and sat down some five yards off to await his turn. Later that night the Big Tigress also came for a feed. Here was a perfect example of the fact that once proprietary rights have been established by the tiger that actually makes the kill, a number of others can feed off the same carcass without unpleasantness. My experience in this and numerous other instances makes nonsense of the old Chinese proverb that two tigers cannot share the same hill. They can and do – although of course a plentiful supply of prey is a *sine qua non* for such tolerance.

In the middle of April a change occurred in the resident tigers' relationships. Tara, having been continuously in the company of her male since the middle of January, now took up with Long Toes, and on the 25th she was spotted by one of her former keepers, Kharak Bahadur. As she crossed a road near the forest boundary, he called out to her, whereupon she sat down to look at him: clearly, she recognised him and his voice just as well as he recognised her. Hearing that she was about, I hastened to the spot with a plate of meat, hoping as always to see her properly, but by the time I reached the scene she had disappeared into the long grass, and when I called, she made no response. Instead, out came Long Toes, who stood listening to my voice, thereby making it clear that he was no less able than Tara's Male to recognise her former companions.

A few days later we had further confirmation that Tara was alive and in the area – and in a manner even more striking than Kharak Bahadur's sighting. One morning I found a fresh tiger spray on the trunk of a small jamun tree near the Leopard Bridge – always a favourite spray-site for my animals. The new spray was about three feet off the ground and five inches in diameter, and a few drops had dribbled down on to the grass. Eelie walked up to the spray and gazed at it for a moment. A puzzled frown creased her forehead, and she ran her nose up and down the blades of grass before doing a token urination on the ground. As she moved away, Harriet advanced, upended her posterior, and deposited her own spray about six inches below that of the tigress. This had been standard procedure when Tara was let out of her cage in the morning, and it left no doubt in my mind that the animals had recognised their former companion from her scent.

Soon the reason for the realignment of partners became clear: a new tigress had appeared on the scene. On the night of April

29 there was a great deal of calling by tigers, and in the morning pug-marks showed that Tara's Male had been in the company of a young female. Knowing of no other young tigress in the area, I thought this must be Tara, although I was puzzled, because I considered she was still a good deal too young to have a family.

Unmistakable sounds of mating started up just after sunset on the evening of April 30, and the moaning whine of the male, punctuated by the roars of the female, continued throughout the night, set off by shrieks of protest from the peacocks, whose slumbers had been disturbed by the explosions of noise.

Next morning it was clear from pug-marks in the heavy dust that the pair had mated, and they appeared to have settled under a jamun tree, surrounded by a thick wall of grass, a hundred yards from Tara's Crossing. Yet also, in the same patch of grass, was Long Toes, who in the night had walked slowly past Tara's Crossing. The way he swivelled his hindquarters from side to side, spraying the bushes beside the road in a release of tension, showed that he was well aware of what was going on – and now, according to all extant literature, the scene was set for an internecine battle, after which the victor would take possession of the bride.

Alas for the theorists, things did not turn out like that. The sounds of mating continued throughout the second day and second night, although the tigers were less noisy than they had been. At some stage in the night Long Toes walked past the courting couple but as the sounds continued unabated in the morning, it was obvious that there had been no unpleasantness.

In his book *The Serengeti Lion*, Schaller records the instance of a lion mating with a lioness while its companion sat watching, about fifty yards away. Then, when he tranquillised the lion which had been performing, the companion took over; and when the tranquillised animal recovered, it assumed the role of spectator. Such behaviour made nonsense of the sensational accounts which claim that the big carnivores fight to the death over an oestrus female – and so it was with Tara's Male and Long Toes. Although the latter was the more powerful male of the two, he went peacefully past the courting couple and continued on his way.

Assuming from my experience with the leopards that the

third day and night would be the last, I tethered baits on two sides of the tigers, west and south, in the hope that I would get a good look at them, and I sat down behind a grass screen covering both sites. Towards midday a rhesus macaque coughed in alarm, and the tigress appeared out of the grass close to the spillway at Juliette Point, but too far away for me to identify her. Ignoring the bait, she went back into some bushes on the other side of the depression. Immediately afterwards her mate called from behind some tall grass to the north.

At once I began creeping as fast as I could to another blind opposite Juliette Point. Just as I reached it, Tara's Male came up the Spillway and walked right past the tethered bait. So close was he that the buffalo retreated to the end of its tether to avoid physical contact, but the tiger ignored it. Even though he had been without food for the period of his mating, and possibly for a large part of his courtship before that, he was still not interested in eating.

As he approached, I suddenly spotted the tigress sitting under a bush on the river bank. I could have wept. This was not Tara at all, but a stranger, with a longer tail and different face-markings. Because she had attached herself to the male between his affairs with the other two tigresses I knew, I christened her the Median.

For a few minutes she continued the intermittent, rumbling aftermath of mating. Then both tigers went into the water for a short while before disappearing up the bank; then a grunt and a muted call from the east revealed that they had gone their separate ways.

After that burst of excitement, the resident tigers settled down to a steady routine. Both males continued to associate at kills, and the tigresses shared them as well. One night Tara's Male killed a bait, and in the morning, because the weather was getting hot, I dragged the carcass into the water to keep off flies and maggots. That night the owner came and fed for an hour at 9 p.m. At midnight Long Toes came, and then in the early hours of the morning Tara's Male came again. Apparently the only concession made to the proprietor of the kill was that when little was left, the remains were abandoned by the others for his personal use.

Another kill, however, brought a new variation. Long Toes killed a small bait, and he and Tara fed; but the next night, when most of it had been eaten, Long Toes left what there was to Tara, who came and fed alone. Such generosity – or maybe one should call it forbearance – did not really surprise me, for I had seen something like it in the behaviour of Harriet, who would not only take a kill to her cubs before feeding herself, even if she was hungry, but would also allow a cub to feed first. Such behaviour is quite different from that of lions, who swat cubs out of the way when feeding.

I was constantly amazed at the way in which the tigers on our home range became aware that there was a kill in the neighbour-hood, and I came to the conclusion that they are extremely sensitive to alarm calls and, probably, death cries, which carry far through the silence of the night and draw them to investigate any commotion. Also, tigers often call to each other and even go in search of one another; and of course a tiger that has made a kill immediately takes news of it to any neighbours with whom he fraternises, in the form of blood and scraps of meat on neck, face and paws.

As I have said, tigers have a very keen sense of smell, which they seldom need to use as their other senses are exceedingly sharp, but I have seen from my own experience that they can follow a ground scent almost indefinitely. One afternoon we dragged a half-eaten buffalo carcass the whole way from Hulaskhani to Tiger Haven – a distance of some four miles – and about five hours later the tigers who had fed on it the night before zeroed in on its new location. I also found that different tigers have definite food preferences: usually only Long Toes and Tara's Male came to the buffalo kills, but one day when Tara's Male killed a chital stag, both tigresses and Long Toes all came to demolish the 150-lb deer in a single night.

At the break of the monsoon in June we stopped baiting, and the Spillway site was flooded. Not surprisingly, the pattern of the tigers' life changed. Long Toes moved away to the north and became a transient; the tigresses also split up, leaving Tara and her male in charge of the range. One day in a raid on a grazing herd east of Tiger Haven, these two killed three cows, of which Tara accounted for one rather stunted animal with a nape bite, while the male got two big animals. This was one of the first kills she had made as a wild tigress, but she soon abandoned it in favour of one of the animals killed by her mate. The fact that she used a nape bite – normally the sign of a confident tiger – betrayed her inexperience: it was a rash grip for a predator of her age to use on an animal as big as a cow.

Soon afterwards the river rose in full monsoon spate and flooded the country round the farm, so that the view from the buildings was reduced to a vista of water with trees sticking up out of it. One morning, as I was having a cup of tea, swamp deer began calling in flooded plains to the south. Evidently a tiger hunt was in progress, and the frenzied alarm calls gradually moved eastwards as the deer milled around in the inundated grassland. Three hours later the noise died down, except for intermittent chital calls in the area of the Croc Bend.

Later I found that the two tigers, in a prolonged amphibious operation, had managed to kill a swamp deer. Not only had they defied precedent by remaining on the low ground, instead of withdrawing to higher, drier areas at the start of the monsoon: they had also used the floods to locate and overcome their prey. Moreover they developed a hunt which would normally have been over in a few minutes into a combined operation lasting more than three hours.

Next night Tara killed a tied-up bait, again with a nape grip; but because of the lack of strength in her jaws, her mouth slipped on the buffalo's neck and one canine drove into the top of its skull. Perhaps because the tooth was slightly injured, she showed little interest in the kill, and went off to finish the last traces of the swamp deer which she and her mate had got after such an effort.

When the monsoon ended Long Toes returned and the former pattern of kill-sharing was resumed. One night Tara's Male took a bait and dragged it across the river; then he tried to pull it up the far bank, but, finding the going difficult because of the piled-up sand, he brought the carcass back into the water and floated it down to an easier landing-place, where he took it into cover. As if to show that the manoeuvre was no fluke, he used the same method on at least two other occasions, swimming with the current and towing a half-eaten buffalo with him.

In October 1978, when Tara was two and a half, she mated with her male over a period of three days and nights in Tiger Copse. I felt sure that she was still too young to conceive cubs, but the tigers' sojourn under a haldu tree, surrounded by a wall of grass, made it perfectly clear what they were up to, especially as every now and then the male gave the characteristic nasal moan. Tara made no audible riposte, and the wooing seemed considerably less tempestuous than usual, perhaps because the bride was still not fully mature. On the fourth day the couple separated, but three weeks later they were together again on a kill, and I listened to Tara calling to her mate as she had called to me while she was dependent on me.

IO

A NOBLE TIGER

At the beginning of 1979 I was lucky enough to witness a
fascinating power-struggle, as a fresh tiger came on the scene
and made a take-over of the range. At first I was puzzled by the
identity of the newcomer, for his pug-marks were highly
distinctive, with the right front foot turned outwards at an
angle, and I felt certain that this could only be Old Crooked
Foot, returned, as it were, from the dead. Perhaps it had not,
after all, been his remains that were found at Bhadraula, but
those of some other tiger. Maybe, during his year of absence, he
had held some neighbouring range, and was now returning to
his former haunts. To avoid confusing the reader, I must make
it clear that in the end the tiger proved to be not Old Crooked
Foot, but his double − Old Crooked Foot II. At the time,
however, I felt sure it was my old acquaintance.

He made his first visit one night in January, when he
approached from the direction of Mutana Tal, and soon he took
to visiting every third or fourth night, walking along the south
bank of the river past Leopard Haven to the Double-Storey
Machan, and there turning left to cross the stream and head
back to the west. On the night of the 23rd he called near
Leopard Haven before making his usual circuit, and from the

increasing persistence of his visits it seemed that he was probing his former range. On the night of the 24th he came to within 150 yards of where Tara's Male was feeding, and though he made no attempt to join in the meal he called three times as he departed, thereby announcing his presence clearly to the other tiger.

Gradually he extended his probe. One evening in February just before dusk, langurs called near the Monsoon Machan and a kakar barked in alarm. After dark another kakar barked near the Escarpment Machan, and not long afterwards the Median Tigress came down off the escarpment near the Jungle Fowl Jetty and killed a buffalo bait at the Leopard Bridge site. After feeding she walked along Am Danda until she crossed the metalled road, whereupon she turned west to go back to her cub – the solitary offspring of her union with Tara's Male. Later in the night she returned for a second feed before again joining her cub. The amount she ate during her two visits appeared to confirm my belief that nursing mothers regurgitate food for their offspring after they have been weaned but before they are big enough to visit distant kills. I had seen Harriet, my she-leopard, do this, and now I felt certain the tigress was doing it too.

Next day we found her pug-marks, together with those of the cub, on a cart-track leading to the river. Evidently she was bringing the cub nearer the kill. We also found the pugs of Old Crooked Foot, who had been down the same track earlier, and had no doubt inhibited her movements. That night only Tara's Male came to the kill: with the natural caution of a nursing mother, the Median stayed away, and the tiger fed alone.

Next day Jackson and I walked down the track along which the tigress had brought her cub. Eelie was with us, and at the mouth of a small ravine she hesitated for a long time before going into the opening. Investigation revealed the pugs of Tara's Male. From another ravine there appeared those of Old Crooked Foot, and at a junction of paths the tracks were superimposed, showing that the two males had fraternised briefly before walking off down the main ravine together. They seemed to get on well with each other: certainly there had been no aggression between them, and I believe the reason may have been that the two were related. Old Crooked Foot was virtually a stranger to the area, both larger and older than Tara's Male, yet he did not try to dominate him by a show of force. If the two were indeed related, they would have recognised the fact from a familial smell, which I believe tigers carry right through their lives.

That night Old Crooked Foot made his first visit to the kill, whose existence he had no doubt discovered from smelling Tara's Male's face in the ravine. Tara's Male reached the kill-site first, and ate a portion of the stomach, but with the arrival of the old stager the atmosphere had evidently turned tense: deeply-indented pug-marks showed where Tara's Male had bridled at Old Crooked Foot's approach, and both tigers had retired without feeding, going separate ways.

Thereafter the kill lay untouched for two days: by keeping apart, the two males had defused a tense situation, and such instinctive behaviour is obviously a means of preventing fatal encounters. When Old Crooked Foot did return, he finished the kill alone. His reappearance seemed to have a disruptive effect: Tara shifted the centre of her range to the grasslands, and her association with Tara's Male appeared to weaken, for he began to disappear over longer periods. Long Toes also made himself scarce: having associated constantly with Tara's Male over kills during the past year, he now took only one bait. Perhaps he too was inhibited by the presence of the older tiger: certainly there is more tolerance among young animals, just as with humans.

On the night of March 10 Old Crooked Foot came from Mutana Tal and killed the bait tied up at Juliette Point. He ate one haunch and left, and though a chital called in the vicinity, showing that some tiger was present, he did not return until after midnight two nights later, whereupon he and Tara's Male both had a feed. The next night Old Crooked Foot arrived alone and did not seem unduly disturbed when I slowly turned on the 1,000-watt bulb, painted red, in the tree above him. Even then, as I watched him feeding, I had no doubt that this was the tiger we had known before.

After his meal he slipped away to cross the river near the Kill

Ford and set off on a further probe towards the Ghulli. What he discovered there was not obvious, but his pugs showed that he came back past the kill and along the Dudhwa–Sathiana road towards Tiger Well at a fast walk, before turning off to the north.

It certainly seemed that the balance of power was being tested by means other than force. Whereas the younger males had found it possible to coexist, the older animal had more difficulty fitting himself into the existing social structure of males and females. A clear sign of the pressure he felt was the fact that the latest half-eaten carcass once more lay untouched for five whole days and nights; only on the sixth did he pull the stinking remains into the grass and feed on them, even though he was in sight of a live bait, freshly tied up. His cautious behaviour was nature's way of enabling him to avoid aggressive encounters.

Lest I be accused of ascribing excessive nobility to tigers, I must make it clear that their avoidance of aggressive postures is a natural spacing mechanism which plays a vital part in regulating the balance of power. Tigers cannot afford to bump into one another unexpectedly, for if they do, their razor-sharp reactions instantaneously trigger the attack response, and the fact that they are so heavily armed may make any confrontation fatal. A human seriously hurt in a fight goes to hospital. A lion injured in a battle with some rival can depend on his pride-mates to let him share their food while he recovers. But the solitary tiger, if hurt, must starve or risk death if he tries to muscle in on someone else's kill. If he cannot retaliate, he is bound to go under to a more powerful opponent, and it is thus, with the aged and the injured being eliminated, that population control is maintained.

I heard typical spacing-calls on the night of March 20, when I sat up once again on the Dimmerstat Machan. At dusk a chital gave an alarm call, and I saw Tara's Male emerge from the grass to the north-east. Langurs started alarm-coughs as he entered the forest, and he called softly three times before ascending the escarpment. Clearly the message was intended for Old Crooked Foot, who soon emerged further east from the same extended grass patch. He seemed in a very irresolute mood. First he entered the river at the Kill Ford and had a drink. Then he crossed the stream, walked towards the Croc Bend, turned back towards the grass patch, changed his mind, headed for the Croc Bend again, changed his mind once more and turned back into the grass. In the space of no more than thirty yards he vacillated and rolled four times and scraped once, leaving a small defecation. He was announcing his presence, but was unsure of himself, as he had never before penetrated this far into the heart of the range.

After passing through the narrow strip of grass he turned right, to the south, and then at some point right again (west), emerging at Chorleekh. Finally he completed his circuit by crossing the river near Leopard Bridge and returning to the kill, the whole manoeuvre being part of the system of spacing mechanics. Shortly before midnight I heard a short burst of explosive roars from near the Monsoon Machan, but other tiger calls, if any, were drowned by the shrieks of roosting peacocks, and after that silence fell. Morning showed that the encounter had been with Tara's Male, but in spite of it Old Crooked Foot had been to the kill and eaten about twenty-five pounds of meat.

The next night he marched down the Sathiana road with long, purposeful strides, keeping a straight course instead of the normal erratic stroll in which a tiger zigzags from side to side. At the turn into Kawaghatia he rolled; then he continued down the slope and crossed the river near the bridge, where we lost his pugs. In the next two nights he completed a huge figure-of-eight circuit which enclosed an area of twenty-five or thirty square miles. It seemed that he had made a full return to his former range.

The events of the next few nights confirmed this – particularly an inspection by Old Crooked Foot of the dimmerstat site, which he crossed the river to look at, as if to show that he was now in charge. Curiosity, however, did not kill this particular cat, and he went on to join the tigresses at a swamp deer kill, which he obviously located from the deer's alarm calls. This kill he shared with the two resident tigresses and also with a stray cub of about a year old, whose pug-marks we had been noticing for the past few months. The animal had been wandering about on its own, and increased my conviction that cubs of a year or more, even if separated from their mother, can survive by attaching themselves to mature tigers.

Also increasingly obvious was that Old Crooked Foot's perambulations now amounted to a full-scale resumption of his former range. Perhaps in younger days he had been able to coexist with other males, but now, crabbed by the intolerance of old age, he could not do so, and even though there had been very little overt aggression, the two younger males had been gradually forced out by a war of nerves. Long Toes paid us his last visit on the night of March 22, after which he disappeared to the north, where he presumably occupied a new range. Knowing him well, I had no doubt that he was fully capable of looking after himself, but some subtle spacing pressure had made him aware that comfortable co-existence with Old Crooked Foot was not going to be possible.

In the same way, Tara's Male was slowly eased out. His visits became less and less frequent, as he was pushed away to the east. For four days early in June he headquartered in the neighbourhood of the Twin Lakes, but after the Big Tigress and her two cubs had made a kill on the night of the 9th, he seemed to lack the courage to come and join them at it. His pugs showed that he came from the east, crossed the Leopard Bridge, and approached to within 200 yards of the kill, but then turned back on his tracks and returned to the Twin Lakes. We suspected that he had made his last journey in daylight, as we heard a monkey call near the Escarpment Machan at sunrise; and later we proved it, when we found the tiger's pug-marks superimposed on the bicycle tracks left by one of my men as he went to get the post.

The next night Old Crooked Foot came from the west and demolished the remains of the kill, before going to spend the day near the Twin Lakes. The night after that he appeared yet again, scavenged the remains, and once more withdrew past the Twin Lakes, crossing the metalled road and the railway line. This was the first time, to my knowledge, that he had ventured so far east, and it seemed clear that he had gone to make sure the other male had left the area, for when, on the fifth day, he returned across the railway line, he called loudly to announce his presence in his domain.

Soon, however, he disclosed a softer side to his solitary

nature. One night he came along the Madrahia road and finished off the stinking remains of an ancient kill. Then he came on to the site where the Big Tigress, her two cubs and Tara had all been feeding on a buffalo. He must have been pretty hungry, for there had been little left of the putrescent remains which he scavenged first, and yet he walked straight past the second kill, leaving the small residue for the cubs.

These – I was sure by then – belonged to him. After other kills he associated with them in the water, and one morning I found him sharing a meal with his family. Yet he appeared very secretive: once when I watched him sitting in the water, he seemed to be deliberately hiding himself behind driftwood, and I could hear him growling very softly to himself. Another evening I sat up over a kill and watched him feed for half an hour, but when I got off the machan at dusk he saw me and ran silently away. This behaviour was strongly at variance with the threat displays mounted against Sid and Jackie Sommers and Dieter Plage; but instead of realising that this was in fact a different tiger, I merely assumed that his earlier ill temper had been caused by the recent gunshot wound in his shoulder, and that now he had become more equable. Certainly he allowed Tara to associate with him, though usually when the Big Tigress was also there; and although Tara seemed nervous in his presence – judging from her running pug-marks – she was obviously also confident that there would be no reprisals as long as she did not overstep tiger protocol.

As Tara approached her fourth birthday, I kept wondering if she would mate with him. In December and January the two were frequently together, and as they indulged in much rolling – a sign of courtship – I concluded that she would soon fulfil her natural function. Yet no mating took place: it was as if natural selection where the dominant male breeds was being blocked by the barrier of Old Crooked Foot's age. At the start of the 1979 monsoon he was certainly well in charge of the Tiger Haven range. Tara's Male had shifted away to an overlapping range mainly east of the railway line, leaving him with an almost clear field. Then, as the rains broke, the kill-sites were flooded, baiting stopped, and the old tiger began to wander extensively.

His pug-marks were found as far west as the Satti monument, and beyond the railway line in the east – a linear beat of about twelve miles. Yet even during these long perambulations he kept returning to the kill-sites, and I began to suspect that, whatever food he might prefer, he was finding it more and more difficult to subdue enough wild prey to satisfy his appetite. My theory was proved by his willingness to devour even the most putrefied kills, long after the tigresses had turned up their noses at them. The evening of his life was drawing in.

His last summer was a strange one, for after a few light showers a drought set in. Although the Neora river maintained a certain minimum flow of muddy water from the hills, it rose and fell considerably below its normal summer level, and the sun blazed down out of a cloudless, rainless sky. This was the beginning of a monsoon failure.

On June 27, 1979, I was walking along the metalled road in the direction of Pallia when I noticed a flock of vultures sitting morosely hunchbacked on a silk-cotton tree, as if mourning the passage of a close relative. Vultures have always fascinated me, for they are the harbingers of death in the forest. When they congregate in large numbers they symbolise the ending of the only life which some animate being will ever know, and the impermanence of existence is never more sharply accentuated than when one realises that the mortal remains of some creature are entombed within those macabre and brooding spectres, which will disappear for ever on the thermals once the feast is over.

I stepped off the road into the tall grass, wet with morning dew, and soon came on a drag which led towards a large and thorny mainphal bush. In some slushy ground I found the twisted right front pug-mark of Old Crooked Foot, the three outer toes indented characteristically in the soft mud. Further on lay the carcasses of two vultures, deep and bloody horizontal welts across their white backs showing that they had been unable to take off in time from under the thick bush as the tiger swiped at them.

The carcass which had attracted them was that of a prime cow. Vultures have been credited with marvellous eyesight, which enables them to discover dead animals from incredible heights, but as this carcass was tucked away under the bush and invisible from above, I could only conclude that the scent of it, rising on a thermal, had been enough to attract them. Clearly Old Crooked Foot had returned to it and surprised them at their meal.

The cow had belonged to a neighbouring village. It had been killed inside the Park buffer zone, where domestic stock were allowed to graze. The villagers knew perfectly well that in taking their herds there they ran the risk of attack by tigers; even so it was quite possible that they would poison the remains of the kill in retaliation. That, I reckoned, was a chance that Old Crooked Foot would have to take. Normal tigers rate cattle fairly low as a prey-species: they do not seem to like the flesh, and prefer deer or pigs. Besides, since they hunt mainly at night, they are not often exposed to the temptations of domestic stock, which are usually herded back into enclosures at dusk. Old Crooked Foot, however, had killed this cow during the day, and there was every sign that with his advanced age, and a possible defect in his teeth or claws, he would continue to prey on cattle in the future. Only a few days passed before he confirmed my diagnosis by killing another cow in broad daylight and dragging the kill into cover.

In a typical monsoon year it would have been impossible for the tigers to go on taking cattle, but now, in the absence of any serious floods, land that would usually have been inundated with water was open to grazing by the myriad scrub cattle which are kept by local cultivators mainly as status symbols – the owners neither kill them for meat nor use many of them as draught animals, so that they are useless except as producers of bull calves. Reports of attacks by tigers kept coming in, and as usual Tara was blamed for all of them. With casualties mounting, I was haunted by the fear that she might be poisoned in reprisal, so I let it be known that I would pay compensation for any animal killed by tigers, even if its death had taken place within the forestry boundary. Soon I paid out 100 rupees – about two weeks' wages – to a man whose calf was killed, even though he brought it on to my land illegally, and more reports of kills began to trickle in.

The morning of October 25 brought a typical claim. Some

graziers arrived to say that a buffalo calf had been killed in the centre of an open field. When I went with them to investigate, I found that a calf had indeed been killed, but in some tall grass inside the forest, from which point the owners had dragged the body about a hundred yards out into the middle of the field, to emphasise the enormity of the tiger's crime and to establish the fact that their herds had been grazing outside the forest. No pug-marks were visible on the hard ground, and vultures had demolished the carcass as soon as it appeared in the open; but the graziers' dishonesty was so blatant that I refused to give them any money, and came away amid dark mutterings.

That evening a thwarted Old Crooked Foot attacked a bullock on its way back from ploughing a field just before dusk. The ploughman, who was following, raised a hue-and-cry, and the tiger abandoned the bullock; but soon it died of its wounds, and no one was any the better for the event, least of all Old Crooked Foot, who remained hungry and on the look-out for another victim.

As the summer wore on it became increasingly difficult for me to convince local farmers that Tara was not responsible for every attack on cattle that took place in the neighbourhood. Much as I wanted her and her associates to survive, I could not afford to pay compensation for every casualty that occurred, and I was glad when the river-level subsided enough for us to resume baiting at the Spillway site. As if to prove that he was not entirely dependent on cattle, Old Crooked Foot arrived there one night, and, finding no bait, proceeded to kill an old chital hind near by. This, however, proved merely a sop to his prodigious appetite, and in the early morning he called repeatedly, as if to register a complaint, from his normal feeding-place, that he had not had enough to eat – though a follow-up revealed that a scapula, a tibia and one hoof were all that remained of the deer.

With the onset of autumn other tigers began to encroach back into the Tiger Haven range. Long Toes came mainly from the north, and Tara's Male mainly from the east, but now another male had appeared as well – a young animal who, I concluded, was probably the singleton cub borne by the Big

Tigress after an earlier mating, when she had mauled Tara, and now a nomad. All the males visited the Spillway site at various times, although Old Crooked Foot was the only one who used the site regularly, and relations seemed to be amicable. Tracks showed that one night he and Tara's Male walked along the yielding sand of the river bank together; the pugmarks of both were almost exactly the same size, but they were easily distinguishable from the old animal's twisted toes, and from his deeper indentations I estimated that he must outweigh Tara's Male by between fifty and a hundred pounds. Again, the male tigers were demonstrating that in areas of prime habitat territorial overlaps are the rule rather than the exception.

One night a bait staked out near Tara's Crossing was taken by Long Toes. Old Crooked Foot, finding nothing at his normal site (the Spillway), crossed the river and joined him; but although the two tigers walked side-by-side at one stage, Old Crooked Foot never visited the kill. The second night the same thing happened, and it seemed almost as if Long Toes was associating with the old tiger in a deliberate attempt to distract him away from the kill.

Peaceful joint manoeuvres continued during the early winter. Normally Old Crooked Foot would lie up in the Leopard Haven Copse during the day. Late in the evening he would call, and then, after a preliminary reconnaissance, would make his way to the kill. I would hear him calling softly as he did the Leopard Haven circuit, and sometimes he would vary his routine by circling the farm before he went to feed. More and more, I sensed that he was under pressure from the younger males crowding in on him.

On the night of February 12, 1980 he opened proceedings with a series of low, rumbling calls from opposite the centre of Tiger Reach, and then strode along the base of the escarpment giving vent to full-throated roars until he was opposite Leopard Bridge, where he went up the escarpment still calling loudly. Then he crossed the river and bypassed the remains of the latest kill to head south. Next morning I found from the tracks that Tara's Male, on his way to the kill, had rolled in a gesture of appeasement near the Croc Bend, but then, hearing the fearsome roars, had thought discretion the better part of valour, and had returned eastwards. Again, the tigers' spacing mechanism had enabled them to avoid a potentially-dangerous clash – and Old Crooked Foot was still in control.

Tara was by then in her second year of freedom, but I had not been able to get a good photograph of her as a wild tigress. Although I knew from her continual presence on the Tiger Haven range that she was alive and well, I needed the proof of it that a clear picture would give, partly for my own peace of mind, and partly to refute the claims of my many denigrators, particularly in the Forest Department, who still maintained that it was impossible to bring up the cub of what they called a 'super-predator' and return it to the wild.

I therefore sought the help of Chuck McDougal, the American expert who for the past ten years had been doing research on tigers in the Royal Chitwan National Park, in Nepal. He obliged by sending down Hashim Tyabjee, a young Indian naturalist, with a battery-operated camera, flash equipment and a remote-control firing device.

We set up the camera within about six yards of a kill, and Hashim withdrew to a machan some fifty yards off, along with a companion who was supposed to share two-hour watches with him. Events, however, did not run to plan, for the companion was afflicted with an unsuppressable cough, which kept the tigers from the kill and Hashim from sleep. However, over the next two nights, a combination of skill and good luck enabled him to get photographs of both Tara and Old Crooked Foot.

These produced a revelation. Tara was easily identifiable from the catapult, or inverted Y, of stripes on the left side of her face and the triangle on her left hind-leg. It was the pictures of Old Crooked Foot that produced the surprise.

The photograph revealed huge callouses on his right forearm, where the limb had been caught in a trap, and suddenly I realised that this was not the tiger who had glared balefully and roared at Sid Sommers. He was big, he was old, and he had been deformed by injury, but he was not the original Old Crooked

Foot. By an amazing coincidence a second tiger with identical characteristics had appeared on the same range. This was Old Crooked Foot's *alter ego*.

As I gazed at the pictures of that distorted limb I felt an ineffable sadness. I could hear the metallic clash as the jaws of the trap closed on it, and the screeches of roosting peacocks as roar after agonised roar rent the primordial darkness. I felt the animal's desperate plunge, and the mighty wrench which eventually freed him. I thought with admiration of the way the great predator had nursed himself back to strength without the aid of social insurance, and of the gallantry with which he had survived to take over the prize Tiger Haven range. I felt ashamed as I thought of the misery which we, in our greed, have inflicted on his race, and of the head-mounted skins, their teeth bared in supplication, which still went through Customs.

The revelation of the reason for the tiger's infirmity increased my natural sympathy for him, and I took to sitting up with Hashim, alternating in his night vigils, to find out more about him. I now realised that he was an exceptionally shy animal.

One night Hashim took a series of pictures which caught Old Crooked Foot in the act of making a kill. Most people believe that tigers attack from the side or behind, but not he: instead, he launched a frontal attack, placed his crooked paw on top of the buffalo's head to force the neck down at an angle and seized the nape in a grip similar to that used by tigresses to carry their young. His method gave conclusive proof that although his right foreleg was misshapen after the punishment it had received, its power was in no way impaired. This kill was shared by Tara, and the next one, made by Tara's Male, was shared by Old Crooked Foot. However, when the Median Tigress and her twenty-month-old cub appeared, he at first chased them away, but later they also fed, and I can only assume that such cautionary chases are part of nature's precautions against crowding.

After Hashim had left, I decided to try to take some flash photographs from the Spillway Machan itself. The project had several disadvantages: first, that the pictures would be taken from well off the ground, and therefore were likely to be somewhat distorted; second, that I had no sophisticated equipment, and thus would be limited by the power of the flash to a maximum distance of fifteen yards, at which range there was a strong chance of being detected by an animal with some of the sharpest ears in the jungle and extreme natural caution.

The night I chose was a dark one, and it seemed that I had sat aloft for an interminable time before a stealthy step in the tinder-dry leaves to the south warned me that my quarry was arriving. A tiger makes a slow, deliberate approach to a bait, and from the direction of this one I presumed that the prowler was Tara. After some time noises of eating began to come from the kill, so I fired off a flash, at which she cantered away. Ten minutes later the same performance was repeated, and after it she went off and sat down to the south of the machan, making a hollow growling, like a dog who does not want his bone yet warns others to keep away.

Soon Tara moved off, and I heard Old Crooked Foot call from somewhere close to the west. Then a somewhat heavier tread told me that the male had come to the kill. I fired off again, and he bounded away, but returned to spit at the source of the flash like the giant cat he was. Five times this performance took place, and by the end he had had enough: he walked off so noisily, in such violent contrast with his stealthy approach, that I could sense his resentment in the swish of the bushes as he pushed through them, to plunge into the river and grunt once in disgust on the far side. Needless to say, I felt thoroughly ashamed of my part in the fiasco, especially as none of the films came out anyway. Though Tara returned to the kill the next night, Old Crooked Foot kept out of the area for two whole days.

By the time the hot weather set in, pug-marks showed that no fewer than four tigresses were frequenting our kill-sites. These, as far as I could tell, were Tara, the Big Tigress and her two sub-adult daughters. One morning stalk along the river proved particularly rewarding: first I found Tara's Male cooling himself in the water. Farther on two females came down into the stream, and farther still Old Crooked Foot had immersed himself in a secluded pool under a fallen log. These daylight sightings confirmed that the two males were quite different in colour: Tara's Male was dark, with a rich orange-and-black coat, whereas Old Crooked Foot was very light, with an off-white dorsal hump.

One evening I sat up on the Spillway Machan. The night was deathly still, the mosquitoes active, the heat oppressive. Nothing happened until ten o'clock, when I heard the muted calls of a tigress on the move to the west, and an answer from Tara's Male further to the north, but by then I had given up hope of the tigers coming to the kill in the early part of the night, and so I climbed down to set off for home. I had reached Shepherd's Machan, about a quarter of a mile from home, when a couple of chital suddenly belled in alarm from close on my right, and no more than fifty yards away round a bend in the track Old Crooked Foot blasted off his spacing-call. I nearly jumped out of my skin – but there was nothing I could do except carry on. Next morning pug-marks superimposed on my own footprints showed that the tiger had turned to follow me and cross the river near the Leopard Bridge.

By then it was obvious that owing to his advancing years and his injury he depended largely on the weekly baits which we provided. Besides, the monsoon, which had just begun, was liable to be a particularly lean period for him, so I decided to continue baiting, even though some so-called wildlife experts maintained that we should not interfere with the natural processes of life and death. To this I replied that we as a race had already tampered with life systems so heavily, and degraded the tigers' habitat so thoroughly, that our management programmes should be heavily weighted in favour of supporting such predators as were left, at any rate until optimum conditions had been restored.

I was away from home for much of that monsoon. After it, Tara's Male emerged for a while from the obscurity in which he had kept himself, but by the beginning of November Old Crooked Foot was once again on his own, and one night I photographed him as he killed a bait with a throat grip. By then he did not seem to mind occasional camera flashes, but after he had finished eating he called in protest as he made off towards Leopard Haven, the resonance of his roars fading into the distance as he voiced his objection to the interference with his normal feeding routine.

He had gradually become a favourite with my staff at Tiger Haven, chiefly because of his bashful ways. They referred to him affectionately as 'Terhua', a vernacular form of the Hindustani for 'crooked', and looked on him as an old but rather demanding friend. One night when he found no bait tied out for him he walked to the Junction Bridge just by the end of the buildings and left his calling card in the shape of a large spray on a tree. Then he crossed the river and sat down on the escarpment, looking across towards Tiger Haven and perhaps wondering who had slipped up. Another night we watched him feeding under the light of a powerful bulb, and when the generator failed I climbed down and left him to finish the feast by himself. We were very close to an understanding, for I am convinced that by then he knew where his prey came from.

And yet the shades of night were closing in on him. He now walked with a limp, and the twist of his right paw seemed more accentuated. It may have been my imagination, but I thought that his spacing-calls as he came to a kill had taken on a hesitant quality. Then one night he killed for the last time: he began feeding from the rump, as usual, but that was the final meal he made on the Tiger Haven range. On the third day Tara's Male came to the kill and the old tiger disappeared, never to be seen again. The younger tiger's takeover from him was not a gradual one, as his own had been, but swift and clinical. Old Crooked Foot, his days of service to the life-cycle over, vanished without a trace. For weeks I tried to discover where he had gone, but the jungles held their secret.

As I view the passing of the years I think often of Old Crooked Foot. I feel the gradual stiffening of the joints, the waning power in the yet-formidable bulk, and the ache in the lacerated forearm when the easterlies blow. Remembering how the young tigers on his range could share their kills, I feel the intolerance of old age and its inevitable consequences of resignation and lack of confidence. I think of the great heavyweight boxers of the past – Joe Louis, Jack Johnson and Jack Dempsey, who never came back, and Mohammed Ali, the Greatest, who did. I wish to think that, like old soldiers, the great tigers never die, but only fade away. Yet I know that even Old Crooked Foot, shrouded as he was in the mantle of his regal past, could not defy the inexorable march of time, and that when he vanished from the range which he had won and lost, he passed into oblivion.

Above *Old Crooked Foot II, showing the huge callous on his right front foot*
Below *R.L. Singh* (left) *with the Median tigress*

11

DEATH OF A TIGRESS

Perhaps I should have been quicker to see danger signals in the behaviour of the Median Tigress. There were one or two incidents which made it clear that she was of uncertain temper, but since they took place when she had a cub with her, I naturally put here aggression down to maternal protectiveness. Now, with the advantage of hindsight, it is possible to see that she was potentially dangerous, but even if we had recognised the fact at the time, there was nothing we could have done about it.

The first incident took place in January 1979, on a day when I happened to be away in Delhi. The tigress had killed a chital and dragged the carcass off towards a patch of dense shrubs. Jackson, doing the rounds in my absence, followed the trail with an accomplice. He was particularly interested, as he and I had recently found the remains of another chital in this very patch of cover, and we had thought that the tigress was making a reconnaissance of the area with a view to installing her five-month-old cub there.

As Jackson approached the site where the tigress had lain up before, he saw a cub disappear into the undergrowth, and heard

Above *R.L. Singh with the stuffed body of the Median tigress which he claimed was Tara. Two years later* (below), *the real Tara, alive and well, comes to a kill in December 1982* the tigress start to growl. Sensibly enough, he and his companion withdrew on to the dirt road, whereupon the bushes shook violently as, with a series of coughing roars, the tigress charged them in a demonstration which brought her to the edge of the track only twenty yards from them. They just had time to walk a few yards along the road when the tigress emerged from the cover to make sure that she had scared the intruders away from her cub.

Returning home next day, I found Jackson somewhat shaken by the incident, and I went with him to inspect the scene of all the excitement. Deep in the bushes we found a small nursery and a few splinters of bone where the tigress had rested, but no sign of her: alarmed by the invasion of her privacy, she had shifted the cub back to the forest block across the metalled road.

During the next three months we frequently came across signs of the family. The Median often associated with Tara, and shared kills with her. By the time the cub was eight months old she evidently judged it big enough to attend kills with her, and several times we found that not only these three, but also the Big Tigress and her two cubs, had all fed from the same source.

In April 1979, there took place another mildly disconcerting incident. Eelie, by then, had grown diffident about coming for walks with me through grassland frequented by tigers; she was still keen to venture into more open country, but, like all animals of advancing years, she knew that her physical abilities had waned, and instinct told her not to put herself at risk. I therefore used to have her on a lead as we set out – both to encourage her and to make sure she stayed close to me; then, as we turned for home, I would let her loose, and she would lead the way back.

That morning she seemed particularly reluctant to come – so much so that she slipped her collar and ran home soon after we had set out. Jackson and I went on alone, and on our way back along a path through tall grass, we saw first the cub and then the Median herself disappear into the cover. I felt very glad that Eelie was *not* with us, and as I sidled past the point at which the tigress had vanished, I saw the outline of her crouching low less than ten feet off. For a moment she scowled at me, and then slid further into the grass. Though she had not growled, or done anything overtly aggressive, I sensed something unusual in the fact that she had stayed so close to the passing humans, and I could not help wondering what had passed through her head during the few seconds she was glowering at me. I thought no more of it at the time – except to reflect on the fact that Eelie had had a miraculous escape.

Nothing else out of the ordinary occurred until the following January. Then, on the evening of the 12th, a labourer on his way home from road-making branched off into the forest to gather firewood and was killed by a tiger. News of his disappearance did not reach the Park Headquarters until after dark, whereupon the Deputy Director and several wildlife guards set out on two elephants, with torches, to find out what had happened. They let off a volley of shots in the area, and afterwards claimed to have seen two tigers mating, but they found no trace of the man. Next evening they returned in a Jeep and fired off more warning shots, but although they saw the body, they did not care to remove it; and when, on the third day, they did recover it, they found that only the genitals had been eaten.

For some reason I did not hear about the accident until this third day, and by the time I visited the site all signs had been obliterated from the immediate area round the kill, but I did find the pug-marks of the Median and her daughter not far off, and I began to suspect the tigress strongly. Even so, the episode was most puzzling, as well as disconcerting. For one thing, I knew that the Median could not have been hungry, since she had fed from a bait killed by Tara only twenty-four hours before the death of the workman. Another odd factor was the Deputy Director's claim that he had seen two tigers mating: it seemed most unlikely that the Median, with an eighteen-month-old cub still at heel, could have come into season already. Besides, mating tigers do not normally hunt at all. I concluded that the Deputy Director had simply seen the Median and her cub together.

Although this was the first human death in the Dudhwa area for some time, there had been many cases of man-eating in other places, and now rumours started flying. Tigers began to be seen everywhere, and one Mintoo, an employee at the Dudhwa tea stall, reported to the Park Director that he had been charged by a tiger while about to answer a call of nature in front of the canteen. He was not amused when I suggested that the tiger had only been trying to maintain sanitation.

Joking apart, the start of the hot weather in April brought an unwelcome development in the form of an outbreak of fires inside the park. By destroying much of the habitat, and reducing the amount of good ambush cover, the fires forced the tigers uncomfortably close together and produced temporary overcrowding, with its inevitable stresses of tension and hunger. The Median took to hanging round the vicinity of the Dudhwa canteen, and when another man was killed near the railway station just before the break of the monsoon, I again suspected her.

At the end of July disaster came nearer home. Again I was away – this time on a trip to London – and when I got back early in August I was greeted with the news that Lallu, my assistant tracker, had been killed by a tigress within a few hundred yards of Tiger Haven. My reaction was one of horror, first at the death of a member of the staff, and then at the thought that the killer might have been Tara. But the evidence produced by Jackson, and a subsequent careful study of pug-marks, established that the culprit had been the Median.

The story of what had happened was pathetically short. At first light on July 30 Lallu had found the tracks of a tigress who had walked along the dirt road to Tiger Haven until she was within a hundred yards of the buildings. Then she had turned round and gone back along the road, to the east. Following her pugs, which he thought might be Tara's, Lallu had gone as far as a small copse just beyond Tara's Crossing. There, without warning, she had leapt out on him as he passed and had sunk her fangs into the back of his neck.

Four hours later, when Jackson went to look for Lallu, he found his axe lying on the track, and a clear drag-mark leading into the grass. The tigress was crouching beside the body and growled at Jackson's approach, but she abandoned the kill when he set fire to the grass. Once again she had eaten only the genitals, but this time it was clearer than ever that her attack had been deliberate. Tracks and flattened grass showed that she had been down by the river, about to cross, when she heard Lallu approaching. She had returned up the bank and crouched behind a tree before launching her spring. The only consolation was that Lallu's death must have been instantaneous, as there was no sign of a struggle.

Now that she had killed three men, the Median had the mark of Cain upon her brow. It was clear that she did not yet regard humans as a normal prey species, for she had scarcely eaten any of the bodies of her victims. Instead of starting to feed from between the buttocks, at the back, as a tiger usually does, she had merely bitten off the genitals, as if confused by the unfamiliar shape of her kill. And yet, even if she had not accepted human beings as routine prey, she was well on her way to doing so, and appeared already to have lost her fear of man.

Because the accident had happened so close to Tiger Haven, the cry went up even more strongly that the culprit must have been Tara. Even the Park Director, R. L. Singh, was loath to accept my word that the Median was to blame. I discussed the matter with him at length, but pointed out that there was nothing we could do until another incident occurred, as six known tigresses were active in the area, and it was impossible to identify any one of them with certainty, either from the pug-marks or from the kind of quick sighting which is all that one normally gets in the wild.

Pug-marks showed that the tigress continued to base herself east of Tiger Haven, between the farm and the metalled road, and that she was often accompanied by her daughter, even though the cub was by then more than two years old – the age at which offspring generally break away on their own. It was clear that neither of them was in any way handicapped: both were perfectly well able to hunt wild prey, and one day in October I came upon the lower jaw and other remains of a chital hind which they had caught and eaten out completely near the Croc Bend.

Then, on November 8, the Median struck again. Late in the morning an old sweeping-woman who worked in the compound of the park headquarters at Dudhwa went off into the teak plantation just outside the perimeter fence to relieve herself. The tigress, who must have been lying up close by, seized her and dragged her down the escarpment into some grass, where she ate one arm and a breast.

The Park Director was away, but instead of coming to me, the staff went out on two elephants to recover the body and bring it back for cremation. Although the rescue-party saw the tigress close to the woman's body, she moved off and disappeared.

For the rest of that day the park headquarters was in turmoil. Nevertheless, at about 4.30 p.m. a man called Asghar who helped look after one of the park elephants went down off the escarpment, where the elephants were tethered in their lines, to answer a call of nature in a deep ravine. No sound escaped him as he was seized, and when his companions went to look for him half an hour later they found his spear and water-container lying in a pool of blood. Evidently the tigress, deprived of her morning kill, had crept into the ravine and lurked there all day, listening to the chatter in the filkhana, or elephant sheds, until such time as the unfortunate Asghar went down to his doom. She had then dragged his body through some thick bushes into a patch of grass.

By the time the news was brought to me, and I reached the scene, it was already dark, and it was impossible to follow the drag. When we did find the body next morning, more than half of it had been eaten. There could now be no doubt about the tigress's motives: the two assaults had been calculated and deliberate; familiarity had bred contempt, and humans were now included in her natural prey species.

Much as I disliked the idea, I had to agree that the first priority must be to kill her as quickly as possible. The Park Director returned post-haste from Lakhimpur, some fifty-five miles away, and the animal was officially declared a man-eater in a radio message from the Chief Wildlife Warden in Lucknow.

With the help of the park elephants I beat the grass near the park headquarters, but the manoeuvre drew blank, so I instructed Jackson to put up a machan above the spot where the man had been killed. That night we staked out a bait there, and

I sat up over it with my ·375 magnum rifle, but the tigress did not return.

Next morning, however, she was heard calling as she moved toward the metalled road leading to Gauriphanta. The Park Director went after her on an elephant, but as he had no armament more formidable than a borrowed 12-bore shotgun, he was scarcely equipped to deal with her. (Later, when we tested one of his cartridges, it failed to go off.) In any case, she emerged on to the road and walked along it for more than a mile, followed at a distance by the elephant, while a messenger was despatched to fetch me and my rifle. As she walked she marked her route in characteristic fashion, swivelling her hindquarters to spray the bushes on either side, and calling repeatedly. By one of the marker posts she turned right and called. She was now on the road along which she had hidden her cub in earlier days and, sure enough, out it came to meet her.

Soon the pair was joined by a third animal. The Park Director thought this was another cub, but I reckon it must have been a stray sub-adult which happened to have joined forces temporarily. All three moved off northwards towards a patch of grass, and the tigress demonstrated against the elephant, standing her ground to cover the retreat of her cub. By the time I arrived the whole group had disappeared, so we tied out a bait at the road junction and withdrew for the time being.

The tigress duly killed the bait during the night, but she could not break the tethering-rope, so at first light we untied it, and during the morning the tigers dragged the carcass into the bushes. This put them in a position advantageous to us, so in the afternoon we mounted a full-scale expedition.

At last the Director had acquired a rifle, an ancient ·375 magnum with a broken safety-catch sent down from Lucknow. I found the fact that he had never fired a shot at a live target rather disconcerting; but since the man-eater was on his territory, it was only right and proper that he should have the 'honour' of despatching it. When I asked if he felt confident of being able to fire a killing shot, he said he had been a good marksman in the days when he trained for the Forest Service. With some trepidation I agreed that he should have the first shot.

He and I mounted one elephant; by special request three American tourists, together with my brother Balram, armed with my own rifle, mounted the other. The hunt did not last long. Following up the drag, we soon came on the kill, of which about a third had been eaten. A few moments later a tiger started up out of the bushes. The Director took aim and would have fired, had I not restrained him and whispered that this was only the sub-adult. Seconds later another tiger rose, only to sit down and gaze at our elephant from a range of no more than ten yards. From her very confidence it was clear that this was the one we wanted, and that she was again covering the retreat of her cub.

Taking careful aim, the Director fired at point-blank range. Balram, from his elephant, saw splinters of wood fly off a branch. The tigress lurched and bounded away without a sound. After giving her a couple of minutes, Jackson scrambled down the tail of the elephant to examine the impact-point and found that the bullet had drilled a hole through an inch-thick branch on its way to the target. There was also the typical flesh deposit of a gut shot. The tigress had been hit, but it was impossible to say how badly: shot like that, she might have gone for miles, and was likely to be highly dangerous.

Jackson got back on the elephant to follow her up. We moved slowly forward, quartering through the thick bushes, and after only a hundred yards we saw her lying on her side, apparently dead. As a precaution I asked the Director to put another shot into her, which he did. Then I got down and threw the empty cartridge case on to her body, to see if it provoked any response. When nothing happened, I resorted to the old hunter's trick of pulling her tail. Still no movement: the man-eater was well and truly dead.

The Director's luck had held to the last, for the branch which he shot accidentally had turned the bullet enough to make it shatter the tigress's heart. Without that deflection, he might have missed her altogether.

The first thing he said, once we knew the animal was dead, was, 'It's Tara, isn't it?'

'No,' I answered. 'It's nothing like her.' That did not stop the Director later writing articles in which he described how I stood there with tears pouring down my face, overcome with grief at the death of my hand-reared tigress.

It is true that I felt a deep sorrow, for I had been instrumental in securing the death of an old acquaintance, who had probably had the chance of killing me many times during my wanderings in the forest. Now she lay dead with a gaping wound in her side. She was perhaps six years old, with no physical defect to account for her fatal predilection.

Everyone climbed down. Photographs were taken. As the excitement subsided, the Director suggested that the best thing to do would be to bury her where she lay, in the forest. 'Excellent,' I said, and I went off thinking that was what he proposed. When I returned to the park headquarters in the evening, I found he had other plans. Now the beautiful tigress lay in a trailer, on a bed of freshly-cut grass, as though deeply asleep, with her ugly wounds covered. The Director had decided to take her on a triumphal flag-march through the principal towns of the district to the State capital of Lucknow, where the Chief Wildlife Warden had his headquarters. I knew that the emotion I felt existed only in my own mind. This was a monster who had sinned not against natural laws but against those made by her destroyers. Even as I watched, the trailer swung out behind a Jeep on the start of its image-building safari, which in due course took in Pallia, Lakhimpur and Sitapur. In every town he played hard to the gallery: the procession stopped for the population to come out and gaze at the slaughtered monster, together with the hero who had conquered her and freed local villagers from their great burden of fear.

Yet the hot air shot off along the way was nothing to that which was generated in Lucknow. There the Director had the whole skin, presented to him by a grateful government, mounted at a cost of 6,000 rupees (about £400, or over two years' wages for an average peasant). Posing beside the stuffed body, he invited journalists in to write up the story. The accounts he gave them were wildly fanciful: soon he was telling people that the tigress had charged him, and in fact he wrote this in an article of his own. In another long article in an Indian weekly he encouraged readers to conclude that the tigress which he had shot was Tara. The fact that it was physically impossible for Tara to have had a cub more than two years old (as the man-eater had) did not apparently deter him from making this ludicrous claim; and as for the fact that the face markings were completely different – this, he said, was simply because such markings change over the years.

12

MAN-EATERS

The death of the Median in November 1980 brought the problem of man-eating tigers into sharp focus for us; yet the fact was that since March 1978 an unprecedented outbreak of man-eating had been raging through the district. Now, as I write at the beginning of 1984, the number of people killed by tigers in Kheri is over 110 and is moving inexorably upwards. The outbreak has caused widespread panic and distress, not least because it is quite unlike anything that India has known before.

It is safe to assume that the killing of humans by tigers has been a fact of life since the beginning of time. There is no doubt that man was once a regular prey species of the great carnivore, along with deer, pig and all the others, for in his time as a primitive hunter he shared the same habitat as the tiger, day in day out. Yet once he settled down to become a farmer, the habitat requirements of the two species diverged, and he ceased to be natural prey. He took to wearing clothes, walking erect, moving in groups, talking loudly, living outside the forest and visiting tiger territory during daylight hours only. Gradually his very unfamiliarity led the tiger to shun his presence.

In those days there was ample room for each species to avoid

the other. The forests were unlimited, and the human population so small that it needed to use only a fraction of the
land-surface. Between the jungles and the pockets of cultivation
were huge buffer areas of scrub and grass. This pattern – idyllic
by today's standards – persisted for thousands of years. Then
gradually the human population expanded, tiger habitat dim-
inished; and in the past few decades the process has suddenly
accelerated with a frightening finality. The buffer zones have
disappeared; commercial exploitation has reduced the forest to a
travesty of its former luxuriance, and humans have returned to
live right on the edge of the jungle or even inside it. As a result,
an entirely new pattern of man-eating has made its abrupt
appearance, brought on by the ecological crisis which we
ourselves have perpetrated.

In the early days of this century, when Jim Corbett was active
in Kumaon, man-eating assumed what might now be called its
traditional form: most tigers behaved normally and avoided
humans, but the few that became man-eaters were forced to it –
in Corbett's view – by the fact that they had been partially
incapacitated by injuries or old age, or a combination of both.

I believe Corbett was right as far as he went, but that there
was also a deeper-lying cause, in the form of local prey shortages. Many of Corbett's killers had been injured by porcupine
quills – but porcupines (as I myself have often observed) are not
at all a favourite form of food, and are eaten only if a tiger is short
of more palatable alternatives. Their flesh is dark and stringy,
and their obvious capacity for defence makes tigers wary of
tackling them. On the occasion when I helped Tara to kill a
porcupine, during her adolescence, I had to encourage her to eat
it. Years earlier, I had watched the male known as the Black
Tiger chase a porcupine all over an area of about an acre,
periodically plucking and spitting out a mouthful of quills,
until he was able to grab the animal by the head; but after this
academic process of killing, he left it.

Old age alone does not turn tigers into man-eaters: if it did,
there would be man-eaters everywhere, eking out their last years
on a diet of human flesh. Nor do wounds necessarily bring about
the conversion. In Kheri one tiger, speared repeatedly in the
rump while caught in a trap, escaped to die of septicaemia and

starvation five weeks later, in the middle of an area inhabited by humans, without having molested anyone at all. Similarly, a sub-adult with a porcupine quill through his lung died of starvation in the centre of a human settlement at Sumerpur, some twenty-five miles west of Tiger Haven, again without harming anybody. Intense compulsion is needed before tigers will take to an alien diet of human flesh. Thus I conclude that the man-eaters of Kumaon were already half-starved when they seized porcupines with impulsive avidity and got their paws and mouths stuck full of quills.

Since then man-eating has occasionally become a major problem in various parts of India, chiefly (again) because of local prey shortages. Kalahandi, in Orissa, and Mandla and Chanda in Madhya Pradesh, have all become notorious for sporadic outbreaks. The only place where it is endemic, however, is the Sunderban swamps in West Bengal. Literally 'Beautiful Forest', this strangely inhospitable land is a mosaic of mangrove swamps swept by tidal waves which surge up the delta from the brackish waters of the Bay of Bengal. Though swamp deer have been exterminated, there is still a plentiful supply of chital and wild pig; yet the harsh ecological conditions have evolved the local tigers into an almost separate sub-species of semi-aquatic marsh-dwellers, and some of them accept the innumerable woodcutters, honey-collectors and fishermen who move among them as normal prey.

In the early 1970s a scientist was sent out by the I.U.C.N. to study the problem. Unfortunately his investigation was interrupted by the Bangladesh war, but in his interim report he identified three different types of Sunderban tigers, and suggested that only some three per cent of the overall population habitually pursue humans as prey. Though far from a blanket condemnation of all the tigers, his work did show that some special problem does exist. He also suggested that a persistent intake of saline water may have caused physiological damage to the tigers' internal organs, and thus induced an acceptance of the human as prey. This idea, however, has been rejected by the Director of Project Tiger, and it certainly seems unlikely that such internal damage should affect only such a small percentage of the tigers, all of whom share the same living conditions. The

Sunderban Tiger Project should continue indefinitely until this unique anomaly is properly understood.

In Kheri, by contrast, there is no mystery about what has set off the present outbreak of man-eating: the reason, in one sentence, is invasion of tiger habitat by humans. Driven out of their ancestral haunts in Nepal by the destruction of the forests there, tigers first built up their numbers in the jungles of northern India, and then overflowed into the crops of sugar-cane which farmers had begun to grow on the newly-cleared land just outside the forest boundary.

The proximity of sugar-cane to forest is extremely dangerous, for to a tiger a field of cane is no different from a patch of tall grass or reeds. There it stands, all through the winter, thick, cool and secure, and in it the tiger takes up residence. As the crop is owned and managed by human beings, it is inevitable that he will come into conflict with them, and that, because he sees them so often, he will gradually lose his natural fear of them.

Many people have asked me why the man-eating should have started *in my area*. I reply that it was going to start *some*where, sooner rather than later, for man and tigers have been on collision course ever since Independence. Nature – the final authority – has at last rebelled against the liberties which humans have been taking in their assaults on the environment, and struck back in spectacular fashion.

The worst-hit area, of some 400 square miles, lies mainly along the Sarda river, which flows south-eastwards through the middle of Kheri. The north bank of the river, once an area of tall grasses interspersed with patches of marsh and stands of luxuriant ratwa and narkul reeds, was the age-old home of tigers, who preyed on the teeming swamp deer, hog deer, wild pig and nilgai that the savannah land supported. In the past thirty years, however, the land has been taken by humans; prey species have been drastically reduced by crop-protection guns, and the tigers' old home has gone.

Such habitat-destruction outside the forest is serious enough; but it was a gross invasion of the reserved forest itself that brought matters to a head. On the creation of the Park in 1977 commercial extraction of timber had come to an end, but resentment over the loss of revenue smouldered on among members of the Forest Department, who in the past had made large sums from illicit commissions on the sales of timber. Thus in September that year, after a great storm had uprooted large numbers of trees, the Department demanded to be allowed to harvest them. At a meeting of the Park Committee in Lucknow I invoked the 1972 Wildlife Act, which laid down that no commercial activity should be carried on inside the Park. By then, however, under the new Janata Government, a move was already afoot to disestablish the Park and return it to the status of a revenue forest, so I knew I was on shaky ground.

Then the Chairman of the Park Committee proposed a compromise: the revenue from the windblown trees should be given to the Park for its development. As wildlife schemes are perennially short of funds, this seemed an excellent idea, and the resolution was passed with enthusiasm. The extraction was to be done by the Forest Corporation (a branch of the Forest Department, which had taken over such work from the former contractors), and the job was to be completed by January 31, 1978.

Soon all hell broke loose in the forest directly behind Tiger Haven, as convoys of trucks disgorged wood-cutters, and the peace was shattered by the sound of axe and saw. Still louder and more penetrating were the yells of the humans, who sought to keep their courage up by making the greatest possible noise, for they looked upon Tiger Haven (where Harriet and Tara were in residence) as the home of ravening monsters. It says much for the equable nature of both leopard and tiger that although the cats' routine was severely disrupted by the invasion, they kept out of the way and did not molest any of the woodmen.

Encampments sprang up along the Neora, and the appalling stench of resident humanity fouled the morning air. I tried to remonstrate for a more subdued atmosphere, but was told to mind my own business, as I had agreed to the extraction in the first place. The operation appeared never-ending. January 31 came and went, and as week followed week, and the trucks ground in and out with their loads of timber, the noise seemed to grow even louder. Then nature joined in the fiesta with heavy rain, so that the trucks bogged down, and the grinding of gears and screams of engines rose to a crescendo. I prayed for the monsoon to come early and halt the whole operation. Before that could happen, however, the tigers themselves took a hand.

One of the sawyers' camps had been established on top of the escarpment overlooking the river bridge at Kawaghatia, some five miles west of Tiger Haven. The inmates included a large number of cartmen, who, with their buffaloes and wooden-wheeled carts, hauled the timber to a relatively accessible dump and stacked it there, for the trucks to take it away. The camp also overlooked the Hulaskhani Bhagar, a low-lying, swampy area famous as the home of tigers.

With their natural prey of deer and pigs driven away by the disturbance, the tigers naturally took to hanging around the outskirts of the camp – for the great cats have a strong attachment to their range – and picking off any of the cart-buffaloes which wandered into the jungle round about. On March 3 a cartman went off to relieve himself near a patch of swamp and narkul, and did not return. His companions, who claimed afterwards to have heard his yells, found his body lying under a bush; about twenty yards away was his loin-cloth, and beside it a pool of blood.

When I visited the scene early next morning, I could see from the pug-marks that it was Long Toes who had struck. A clear drag-mark ran from the loin-cloth to the spot where the body had been found. Though the men said the victim had been seized in the open while cutting grass – implying that the attack had been deliberate and cold-blooded – it was fairly obvious that he had been taken while answering a call of nature, as his loin-cloth was lying in a tidy heap and was not stretched out, as it would have been if it had been scraped off him as he was dragged along the ground.

Of course there was an immediate clamour for the tiger to be declared a man-eater and shot. The only person empowered to issue such a declaration was the State Chief Wildlife Warden, who mostly operated from his office in Lucknow, 150 miles away, and on this occasion he decided not to visit the scene of

Above *Death of a man-eater: the tiger shot at Ghola*
Below *Tara on a kill, April 1981, her left cheek catapult-mark clearly visible*

...d tigers mating: a unique ...ence. Opposite: above, the ...arches in display to a ...nbent Tara; middle, the ...ing couple rub noses in the ...; below, pause for reflection: ...reat size of the male shows ...ly. Right: above, Tara rolls ...ocatively while the male ...res for action; middle, the ...about to mount, with mouth ..., below, copulation takes ... The act is repeated many ...during the mating period, ...h lasts up to three days.

the accident or to take action. In a letter designed to smooth things over I told him that, as the tigers' prime habitat had been utterly disrupted for the past three months, I was surprised that no accident had taken place sooner. I also added that I felt sure the man had been taken while squatting down, for, as more and more records show, tigers usually take humans from a crouching or sitting position, presumably mistaking them for quadrupeds.

In any case, the local clamour gradually subsided, but the cartmen refused to stay anywhere near Hulaskhani, and shifted their camp to a site below the Dudhwa Forest Rest House. Here it only needed a tiger (shown by the pug-marks to be Tara's Male) to seize a buffalo near the Twin Lakes one afternoon, and the rout was complete. The men packed up and pushed off elsewhere.

The next incident took place near Ambargarh, a former border post just west of Kawaghatia, now abandoned because the forest guard on duty there was once set upon by robbers. Ambargarh used to be deep in the jungle, but the forest on the Nepalese side of the border had been cleared for agriculture and former soldiers had been settled on the land. When Jackson lived for a few days in one of the settlements during a search for Prince, the leopard, in 1975, he found that almost every hut contained at least one firearm – presumably illicit, and used to slaughter local wildlife.

The people of Ambargarh had long since made free of the forest on the Indian side of the frontier, penetrating deep into it to graze their cattle, cut wood, poach, fish and so on. On April 3 one of them failed to return home. He had gone out into the forest – it was alleged – to look for cattle. A search-party found his mortal remains on the bank of the Neora river, and carried away all that was left of him – his rib-cage – for cremation

Once again I was summoned to help, and when I visited the site next day I found that although the actual killing had been done by a male tiger – not Long Toes – a tigress and two small cubs had left their pug-marks in the mud at the entrance to a small water spillway where the man had been surprised. This

Above *Tara cooling off in the river, May 1982*
Below *The conference: Tara and her first litter of three cubs in the river*

discovery clashed with the widely-held theory that a tigress always keeps her cubs away from their father, and appeared to confirm my own belief that in times of stress a male will kill for his family. Again, in spite of the local outcry, no official action was taken.

Only three days later, on April 6, the tiger struck once more. Another Nepali went off alone into the forest, by one account to cut grass, by another to graze his buffalo. Whatever his purpose, he entered the jungle illegally, and on his own. He too failed to return. Next morning a search-party set out to look for him, including the Park Director and some armed guards, and from one of their vantage-points, up a tree, they actually saw the tiger (a male) at his grisly repast. Even though they yelled and threw branches down on him, he dragged the remains of the body away into cover. Both the Park Director and the Chief Wildlife Warden clearly knew that the man-eater was a male, and yet both declared that the culprit was my hand-reared tigress.

When Jackson and I visited the site next day, we again found the pug-marks of the tigress and her cubs. Whichever animal had done the killing, the mother had fed on the kill as well. The man's scythe was still lying beside a bundle of cut grass, and on its blade were a few severed hairs from the tiger's coat, showing that he had made a desperate swipe at the animal as he was being seized. By then there was no trace of the body, which we assumed had been completely eaten.

Another furore started, and the Park Director was heard to remark that if it had not been for the authority of his superior, the Chief Wildlife Warden, and the threat of retribution, he would have shot the tiger himself. This kind of attitude and hasty reaction were exactly what I most disliked: the Park Director ignored the peculiar circumstances which had driven the tiger to start killing humans, and would clearly have preferred to eliminate the animal, rather than trying to work out some way of saving it. The one consolation was that the tigers had succeeded in sealing the international frontier, which the paid border staff had been unable to do, and they had struck a powerful blow for the sanctity of their own habitat.

Since there was obviously a shortage of wild prey in the area, and as the male was killing for a tigress with cubs, I suggested that we should try to tide them over this period of maximum stress by supplementing their diet with a few buffalo baits. The Park Director said he would consider the idea, but before he came to any decision another fatality occurred.

This time the victim was a Tharu tribal – a somewhat simple-minded fellow, who strayed into the forest on April 27 near Kiratpur, two miles from the previous kill-site. As usual I was summoned to give advice and help, and when I arrived the morning after the man had disappeared, I found that no attempt had been made to recover his body. Together with Jackson and an Assistant Wildlife Warden I went to the place where the man had been seized, and began to follow up the drag, which crossed and re-crossed the dry, winding bed of the Neora river. The pug-marks were those of a male. Presently, beneath a bush, we found an arm, and a patch of blood where the body had been eaten during the night. From there, I was surprised to see, a tigress had taken over the drag. Following up further, I found the pug-marks of a small cub in the sand on another bend of the river – and there, with its features set in a hideous grin of death, was the tonsured head of the victim, cleaned of all hair by the tigress's rasping tongue. Leaving the grim relic where it was, I returned to the settlement and told the villagers to collect it, but I doubt if they ever did.

It was quite clear that the same family of tigers had been responsible for this latest kill; equally clear, from the lack of hoof-slots, was the fact that the area contained very few ungulates, most of them having been shot by villagers or driven away by the disturbance of timber operations. If we were going to save these tigers, and at the same time forestall further human casualties, we had to take positive action.

To my great relief the Park Director at last consented to provide baits at public expense and tie them out on selected sites. For the next six weeks or so the tigers killed and ate them regularly. To get an idea of what was happening I spent much time patrolling the area on foot, and during the hottest part of the day I several times saw the male tiger sitting in the waters of the Neora or the Nagrol. The first time I came on him, he fled, but gradually his confidence grew, and after a while, even if he spotted me, he did not react aggressively, but would remain immersed to his eyebrows in the river.

I was glad to find that our experiment proved entirely successful. To cut short a long story, the man-eater was reformed, and never again killed a human being – not that official accounts of the episode ever admitted any such heresy. Dogma maintained that attempts to reform man-eaters were a waste of time, and ignored what had happened. Even so, I had the private satisfaction of seeing the tiger restored to a normal existence, and of watching the tigress continue with the education of her cubs – by then well grown – during the next winter.

The issue was clouded by the fact that another outbreak of man-eating began in the middle of the monsoon at the start of August, 1978, in farmland immediately outside the park. On August 1 a fifty-year-old man was taken while cutting grass outside a field of sugar-cane, and on the following day his body was found partly eaten. Farm dogs began to disappear, and then, on August 7 another man was killed. Again the tiger had been in a field of sugar-cane through which it was said to have stalked the latest victim.

The killer, thought from the size of its pug-marks to be a tigress, was declared a man-eater, and the Forestry Department took steps to deal with it. To their credit, they did not set out to shoot it outright, but at least made an attempt to dart it with a tranquillising gun, their aim presumably being to put it into a zoo.

The events that followed, though tragic, took on farcical overtones. A bait was staked out, and on August 11 it was killed. The remains were dragged under a tree, in the hope that the tiger would return, but it never appeared. When a second bait was taken three days later, a Wildlife Warden ensconced himself on a machan armed with a dart-gun and accompanied by a local farmer who had an unlicensed rifle.

After waiting there for some time, they suddenly saw a tiger stalking through the edge of a field of sugar-cane beside the road. At the same moment some children on their way home from school were approaching on bicycles. The men shouted out that the tiger was there, whereupon the children threw down their bicycles and ran back the way they had come. The tiger continued walking, as before. The forest officer, who was untrained in darting procedures, dutifully fired off his gun when the target was still some 150 yards away. Needless to say, the low-velocity dart, with a maximum effective range of about forty yards, plunged into the ground far short of its objective, whereupon the farmer shot the tiger with his rifle and killed it.

The animal turned out to be a young male, in perfect condition. The fact that the man-eater's pugs had been diagnosed as those of a tigress was conveniently forgotten, and the dead tiger was proclaimed to be the very animal which had been active at Sathiana and Ambargarh in the spring. An official report blandly stated that this was indeed the Sathiana man-eater, ignoring the most obvious facts – first, that the Sathiana killer was a full-grown male, much bigger than this one, and second, that to reach the area of the August killings it would have had to traverse about twelve miles of heavily-flooded land, with almost no prey animals on the way.

It seemed much more likely that the young tiger had been washed down-river from Pilibhit in the heavy monsoon spates – something that happens frequently – and, finding himself suddenly in a strange area, had had to subsist on whatever he could scrounge, for he had been killing dogs and chickens. But as Government statistics had to be kept up, the easiest thing to do was to tidy up the books by entering the shot animal as the Sathiana man-eater – for dead tigers tell no more tales than live ones.

From the moment the Kheri tigers began killing people, Tara was constantly accused of being the villain. Even when it became clear that several different tigers were involved, there was still a loud clamour for her blood. No one was more ready to damn her than 'Tootoo' Imam, one of the shikar outfitters who had lost almost all their business when the ban on hunting was introduced. Now he was encouraged to visit Dudhwa, with visions of reviving his commercial operation. Certainly people were prepared to part with vast sums for the privilege of shooting a man-eater: one foreign client is said to have offered two lakhs of rupees (200,000 rupees, or some £13,000) for a single shot. Imam staked his reputation as a tracker on his announcement that most of the thirty-odd human kills which had taken place so far were the work of Tara.

Nonsense though this was, particular tigers began to be declared man-eaters without proper evidence or evaluation. The fact that the first animal destroyed turned out to be a male took the heat off Tara temporarily, but then three females and two males were shot in rapid succession, including a pair which were admitted to have had no record of man-killing.

This last incident was particularly regrettable. Early in 1979 I was invited to investigate the operations of a man-eater in and around the Barauchcha Nala, an isolated area of remaining habitat, cut off in agricultural land. When I arrived there I was told that a particular tigress had killed a buffalo bait and had been earmarked for destruction. As I had also been told that there were five tigresses in the area, I asked how people knew which one of them it was that had killed the man: there was no reply, but the question was not a popular one, and I was not invited to help any more. I also heard that there was only one male in the area, known as the Sant, or Holy One, who had never harmed anybody. Yet in the politically-motivated witch-hunt that followed both he and a tigress with no man-eating record were exterminated.

So little was being understood of why the man-eating had broken out, and so great were the slanders being heaped on Tara, that in February 1979 I invited H. M. Patel, Finance Minister in the Janata Government and now Chairman of the Indian Board for Wildlife, to visit Dudhwa and make his own assessment. He was met by an impressive deputation of locals seeking protection from tigers, and local bus-owners staged a meeting to express sympathy for the travelling public. The upshot of the visit was the appointment of a committee from Project Tiger to investigate the problem and suggest a remedy. Needless to say, I was not invited to be a member.

The committee – and the report it produced a year later – were little short of disaster. The leader was S. R. Choudhury, one of Project Tiger's Field Directors, and owner of the famous pet tigress Khairi, described as 'the topmost living authority in the world on tigers'. His fitness for taking charge of the inquiry was hardly increased by the statement that he personally had destroyed more than fifty man-eaters, and when his verbose and highly conjectural report appeared, it recommended that 'socio-ecological conflict' between the tiger and the local population should be solved, whenever it broke out, by the elimination of the tiger, as expeditiously as possible, even if it involved killing the wrong animal. Choudhury also recommended poisoning as a permissible means of destroying tigers, and suggested that they could once again become useful as a commercial resource (that is, if shikar clients were allowed to shoot man-eaters).

Although he did admit that habitat had been degraded, and that wild prey species had been severely depleted, he also made the confused statement that one result of tigers living in a restricted environment was that they were increasing 'contrary to Malthusian principles'! A more sensible – if vague – suggestion was that 'Tiger watch' teams should be established – small, mobile units, with specialised knowledge, which could proceed quickly to any new outbreak and analyse what was going on with some degree of expertise.

Another idea was that man-eaters might be captured rather than shot. Capture is something which I myself advocate – but only provided that the aim of the operation is to transfer the captive to a more suitable wildlife habitat, rather than to confine it in a zoo. As I explained in my account of the Banga Jhala fiasco at the beginning of the book, no tiger which has lived wild has any chance of surviving for long in a zoo: it is therefore a waste of time and money to trap man-eaters with the idea of putting them behind bars, for one is only condemning them to a slow death.

Not that this well-known fact deters those who see incarceration as the easy way out of a problem – as one more example will show. On the night of March 10, 1983 a trap was set up and camouflaged in a farmer's cane-field just outside the Park boundary, only three miles from Tiger Haven. The quarry was a tigress suspected of having killed a man, but the hunt for her was complicated by the fact that a whole family of tigers was active in the same area – a male, the female, and two well-grown adolescents. The trap was baited with part of a kill on which all four had fed the night before, and at eleven p.m. one of them entered the cage.

It was typical of the haphazard way in which such operations are set up that no tranquillising drug was immediately available. The only man capable of administering such a drug was the Research Officer of the Corbett National park, who over the past two years had found it very difficult to tranquillise any tiger, and now was away at headquarters in Lucknow so that he did not reach the scene until 3 p.m. next day. By then the trapped tiger had been in the cage, untended, for sixteen hours; word of its capture had spread, and a vast crowd – estimated at 10,000 people – had poured out of Pallia and from the surrounding villages and farms to stare at it.

True to form, when the Research Officer eventually arrived he proved unable to sedate the animal with his dart-gun, so that he had to go right up to the cage and use a hypodermic syringe. Needless to say, the animal was badly injured in its struggles to escape, both before and after the Research Officer came on the scene.

At last, after rendering it unconscious, he took its temperature by lifting its tail and inserting a thermometer in its anus; having done this, he announced that the animal was a male, and that the female would have to be captured as well, as she was the suspected man-killer. The tiger was then taken off to Lucknow Zoo, and it was only there that the animal was declared to be a tigress. The sexual organs of the male are so prominent that it seemed scarcely possible for the Research Officer to have made such a mistake; and yet, incredibly, the zoo maintained that he had. I hardly need add that the killing continued as before: the Forest Department, having failed to identify the man-eater properly, condemned an innocent animal to penal servitude and (as it inevitably turned out) death. The captive, named Preeti by the zoo, died there on October 23, 1983 after a slow decline – as did Basanti, another captive tigress from Naini Tal, who died of 'snakebite'.

To say that I was taken aback by these developments would be to put it mildly. Here was a clear instance of local authorities defying the clearly-stated law and ordering the imprisonment of an animal which they knew perfectly well would not survive. Their excuse was that they were trying to appease local anger and fear – and of course they advanced the specious argument that by putting the animal behind bars they were 'saving' it.

No action was taken as a result of the Choudhury report, and casualties continued to mount. By February 1981 the total had passed sixty, and at a meeting of the Indian Board for Wildlife in Delhi, under the chairmanship of Mrs Gandhi, I suggested that a body should be set up immediately to investigate causes and suggest remedies. A strong committee was accordingly formed, with H. S. Panwar, the new Director of Project Tiger, as Secretary, but as the body had the additional mandate of reporting on the feasibility of reintroducing hand-reared predators into the wild, it was natural to exclude me. A year later they submitted a lengthy report, in which they stressed that the main reason for the man-eating was undoubtedly the pressure of human population on habitat areas. Among the short-term remedies they suggested were the establishment of Tiger Watch teams for monitoring the movements of potential man-eaters, the speedy removal of 'proven aberrants', changes in the old system of harvesting grass and firewood, and the payment of compensation for the loss of human life and cattle. Long-term suggestions included the creation of a much larger tiger reserve, which would include not only Dudhwa but also two other core areas of South Kheri and Pilibhit, and the establishment of long forest corridors linking one block with the next. They also suggested the diversion of some road and rail links to take them outside the National Park.

Of these proposed measures, the only one so far implemented is the payment of compensation for human deaths. Yet the amount is still derisory: 5,000 rupees, or about £300. Nothing has been done to combat the menace of tigers living in sugar-cane.

To emphasise the havoc which can result if tigers do take up residence in a cane-field, I will relate one more series of incidents in which I became involved during 1983. This took place at Ghola, a 3,000-acre area of buffer land immediately outside the Park opposite Sathiana. Once the favoured haunt of the swamp deer, it has now been cleared and cultivated, and during the winter months tigers live in the sugar-cane which has been planted right to the boundary of the forest.

One night late in May a tiger walked up to a watchman guarding his crops and seized him through his quilt, under which he was sheltering from the cold. Fortunately the man's lantern overturned and set fire to some straw, and the tiger decamped.

Some time later, by an amazing coincidence, the same man was again seized by the same tiger while he was stripping cane. This was a daytime attack, and he was saved partly by the fact that the people with him shouted, partly by the fact that he had a large piece of cloth wound round his head, so that although he suffered a severe scalp wound, he was not fatally injured – thus possibly creating a record as the only man who has twice escaped from the jaws of the world's most powerful predator.

Soon after this another man came with his wife and child to visit some friends late one afternoon. As he squatted to urinate by the edge of a field of sugar-cane, a tiger seized him and dragged him into the crop. His friends set fire to the cane to scare the tiger off, but by the time they drove the tractor into the half-burnt field, they found only his dead body.

Naturally the local people were upset and frightened by the death; but the situation was aggravated by the fact that the owner of the ruined sugar-cane, who lived away from his fields, was unable or unwilling to realise how terrifying existence became in a place where a tiger had accepted humans as a legitimate form of prey. Instead of sympathising, he demanded redress for the loss of cane he had suffered.

When I arrived on the scene next morning, I was assailed by demands that the animal responsible for the crime should be eliminated immediately; the people told me it was a tigress but, on visiting the site of the death, I found the killer to be a male. When the locals sought to assert their rights to the area by saying they had lived in it for ten years, I did not endear myself to them by replying that tigers had lived there for over a thousand. Stories about Tara had already made me unpopular, and now the old women of this apparently-matriarchal society threatened to assault me, on the grounds that I had started this wave of killing by introducing a hand-reared tigress to the National Park: a whole crowd of them surrounded us, screaming threats and abuse.

Next morning the tiger struck again, seizing a girl outside her hut about a mile away: she too was dead by the time her body was recovered. A few days later a man went out to level his field in preparation for sowing: he had two buffaloes yoked to a plank, on which he stood both to steer the animals and to make the levelling more effective. The buffaloes were working up and down at right-angles to a field overgrown with short green grass, alongside which was a stand of tall sugar-cane. As they turned away from the grass field, the tiger launched an attack on his selected prey: he seized the man and, without pausing to kill him, began dragging him into the cane. Rescuers rushed shouting to his aid, and he was still yelling as he was borne off, clamped in the jaws of his destroyer; but although the tiger left him, he died soon afterwards.

As usual, local agitation engineered by political aspirants started up, and a farmer who had earlier complained about Prince, my leopard, wrote to the Prime Minister saying that unless action was taken by the Forest Department, he, after a token fast of a week, would shoot the offending tigers himself. As a result, a tigress was declared a man-eater (even though I had made it plain that the culprit was male), and the Director of the Dudhwa National Park was entrusted with her destruction.

He therefore put up a machan on a handy pipal tree and started sitting up over a live bait. One night the bait was killed, but unfortunately the Director happened to have gone away, and the tiger ate most of the small buffalo. Next night the tiger arrived soon after nine p.m. to finish his meal, but the remains had been carelessly tethered, and he broke the rope and started to drag the carcass off into a nearby patch of sugar-cane. The Director fired a hasty shot, which (I found on inspection in the morning) missed. Later that night the tiger returned and dragged the kill right away.

By now terror had gripped the entire community, as the people, living in their fragile, isolated huts, realised how vulnerable they were to a resolute tiger who deliberately sought the human being as prey. Fears were redoubled by the knowledge that the killer had not made a single meal out of his last five human victims; thus he had killed more people than he had needed to satisfy his hunger, and would certainly strike again if not shot first. Soon he would be bold enough not to relinquish his kills when challenged.

The Forest Department was blamed for not taking serious steps to destroy the tiger, but most of the anger was vented on me: the people complained that I was protecting and encouraging the tigers, and that the man-eating had only begun since I released Tara. They also claimed that they were now haunted by the spirit of a local farmer murdered years before in a land dispute, which had taken up residence in the body of the tiger, and could not be destroyed. In spite of my point-blank assertion that the killer was a male, the wildlife officials still maintained it was a female – no doubt hoping that if they managed to shoot a tigress, they would be able to claim that they had despatched the hated Tara.

That evening another bait was tied up, and the Director again took his place on the machan. At ten p.m. the tiger charged out and grabbed the buffalo, but instead of waiting until the killing process was over and he had a steady target, the Director fired another hasty shot, without any definite conclusion. Next morning he came looking for me in a panic, and asked me to take temporary charge of the hunt. Having driven home to collect my rifle and Jackson, I proceeded to the scene. As we started investigations, the atmosphere was tense, and scathing references to the ineptitude with which operations were being conducted ceased only when Jackson found a faint smear of blood. We then began the unpleasant task of trying to locate a wounded tiger inside the dense sugar-cane.

As there was zero visibility inside the cane-field, it was too dangerous to follow up on foot so we assembled a party of four elephants. We found that sometime during the night the tiger had emerged at the far end of the field, but had turned back on his tracks into the shelter. There we found a few more blood-smears; the unsheathed claws visible at the front of the left forepaw pug-marks showed that the wound was in the left front leg, and severe enough to make the animal shy away from venturing out into the open.

For some time we combed the field with the elephants, until suddenly, from almost underneath one of them, a tiger gave a harsh snarl. The realisation that he was still very much alive

shook many of the searchers, and instantly a vociferous argument broke out about what should be done next. I said that, as
we had now located the animal, we must not lose touch, but
should close in and try to finish him off. Others, however, began
to edge away from the spot in which the tiger was lying, and the
badly-trained elephants started fidgeting nervously.

I became exasperated and since the operation was supposed to
be under the control of the Forest Department, and I could not
give orders about what to do, I decided to stand down from my
position as temporary leader. Then someone advanced the
suggestion that a tractor with a levelling plank should make
lanes through the cane to improve visibility. This entailed a
two-hour wait for a machine to be fetched, and the lethargy of
inaction took over. By the time the tractor had at last come, and
opened up a few lanes, the owner of the field also arrived and
objected strenuously to the havoc being wrought in his crop, no
matter how worthy the cause.

Once more everyone withdrew from the cane-field, and a
temporary stalemate ensued. But soon temperaments flared: the
owner of the field slapped the tractor-driver. The tractor-owner
took umbrage and fired a smooth-bore shot at the farmer,
although fortunately from a distance. For a while a fight
between two factions of the Sikh community seemed imminent.
No sooner had peace been restored than local settlers attacked
the Sikh farmer with sticks and stones for not letting his field be
levelled. When he leapt into a Jeep and drove off, they brought
matters to a head by setting fire to the crop.

As the vaulting flames leapt through the cane, the tiger was
seen limping slowly and painfully across one of the lanes, and it
became clear that he would not leave cover until he had to: only
when the field had burnt right out would he emerge. The
elephants shifted uncomfortably as tongues of fire flickered on
the skyline. Sensing what the end would be, everyone who was
armed dismounted, except for the Park Director, and formed a
line across the north-eastern end of the field, where the blaze was
obviously going to burn out.

The firing squad's formidable armament included three ·375
magnum rifles, one ·30-06, two ·315s and an assortment of
smooth bores. The marksmen formed the front line, and

immediately behind them about two hundred local inhabitants waited eagerly for the grand finale. As the flames approached, the heat became intense even where we stood, away from the edge of the crop. In the end only one small triangular patch remained unburnt; and just as people were beginning to fear that in some mysterious way the tiger had managed to double back, two shots rang out from the Park Director and his accomplice, whose fidgeting elephant was some 200 yards off. Their only effect was to turn the tiger back into the cane, but at last he emerged in front of us with a defiant snarl.

At the first two shots he buckled and went down. Then he staggered to his feet again, but when I fired he crumpled and collapsed. A great cheer rent the air, and everyone began firing wildly in a *feu de joie*. The release of the enormous tension was palpable. The Assistant Wildlife Warden, carried away by excitement, ran forward still firing, even though I yelled at him to desist. Rushing up to the fallen tiger, he seized it by the tail and then, to show how little he feared it, launched a violent kick at its head (I was glad to see that next day he was limping, and the day after that had his foot in plaster.) The women who had previously threatened to assault me now hastened to garland me with tinsel, crying our 'Arjan Singh *ki jai*!' – 'Praise be to Arjan Singh!' Their sudden and violent change of mood reflected all too clearly the state of terror to which the man-eater had reduced them.

The man-eater of Ghola was an average-sized male in his prime, with no serious infirmity. A post-mortem revealed that the first shot had broken his left shoulder, and under his skin, healed over, were several charges of buckshot. Yet he had never been incapacitated. His sudden acceptance of an alien prey species, which had led to five human deaths and an incalculable amount of fear and stress, had been caused simply by the fact that he had been thrust into proximity with mankind – an accident in no way his fault. Culpable though he was in human terms at having become a murderer, I could not suppress a pang of remorse at his passing.

If men and tigers are to coexist in amity once again, humans must separate themselves and their activities from tiger territory. To achieve such a separation, I believe that a ten-point programme is needed, and that the following innovations must be made:

1 Compensation for loss of human life should be increased at once to a more realistic figure. Compensation for loss of domestic stock to tigers should be paid promptly.

2 A buffer zone free of sugar-cane five miles wide should be instituted round the Dudhwa National Park. In this zone farmers would be paid *not* to grow cane, and would be encouraged to plant short crops such as wheat, barley and mustard which would be inhospitable to tigers.

3 An electric fence should be erected round the periphery of the park, to keep prey species and predators within the park.

4 People living near the boundary should be provided with single-phase electricity, to give them light at night. Isolated hutments should be consolidated into villages as a protective measure. Government assistance should be made available so that these people can build houses. They should also be provided with bio-gas cookers fuelled by methane generated from cow-dung. Such measures will cut down the huge annual demand for thatch, other natural building materials and firewood which now draws thousands of people into the park each winter.

5 The park should acquire 3,000 acres of land at Ghola and allot the people who have settled there alternative land.

6 In the Sathiana grasslands the habitat should be improved for the swamp deer — the main tiger prey species in the area — to encourage them to remain there during the rains.

7 A special Park Cell should be formed to monitor tiger movements and deal with individual cases of man-eating as they come up.

8 A survey should be made of the northern area of the Park to improve degraded habitat and encourage tigers to move back there. This northern sector was once prime tiger habitat, but has ceased to be so because of human intrusion and grazing by cattle, with the result that the main tiger population is in the south.

9 No human activity should be permitted in areas of tiger residence; if humans do enter them, it must be understood that they do so at their own risk.

10 Single persons should be forbidden to enter any area frequented by tigers. If humans have to enter such areas, they must go in groups.

Some of these measures obviously apply only to Kheri, but the majority should be put into operation round all India's tiger reserves. Such schemes, it may be argued, will demand formidable organisation and expense. I agree. But in trying to save the tiger we have taken on a formidable task, and unless we are prepared to adopt bold and imaginative steps in our attempts to tackle it, we shall lose the battle.

Man-killing must be seen – and treated – as an ecological reaction to the gross over-exploitation of natural resources carried out by humans in the past thirty years. Shooting tigers is no answer to it. (Jim Corbett, had he been alive, would have been the first to point this out.) Shooting may be the easiest short-term solution, particularly for the vote-catching politician; but it must be recognised that the problem is no less an ecological catastrophe than the collapse of hillsides undermined by quarrying or the flooding of river basins caused by forest clearance in the hills and the consequent erosion of topsoil. The only long-term solution will be the kind of separation I have outlined. Until then, the killing of humans in and close to forest areas must be regarded as an occupational risk.

Unless proper separation is achieved, we shall rapidly progress from a situation in which most of the deaths result from the accidental confrontation of tiger and man, to one in which more and more tigers accept humans as a regular prey species and become compulsive man-eaters. If that happens, we shall be in a really dangerous position, for not even an abundance of other prey will prevent human deaths. Another consideration is that as long as the tiger population can spill out of the forest into the cane-fields, it will continue to increase. Only if the predators' living-space is restricted will their own automatic systems of population control – fights, smaller families and so on – come into action.

Though Kheri has had the most acute man-eating problem to date, other areas will soon experience the same thing unless positive action is taken. Already some enormous operations have been put in hand to remove humans from the tigers' habitat. In Simlipal, for instance, there is a huge project to move 2,000 families, consisting of 12,000 people, out of the core area of the park and shift them bodily on to fresh ground

Above *Tara's Male disputes a kill with turtles*

outside. In the first phase alone about 1,000 families from nine villages were resettled. Eight villages have been moved out of the Ranthambore reserve. Such is the scale on which remedies must be taken.

At the time of writing, however, little has been done in Dudhwa to implement the findings of the man-eater committee. Plans for a Tiger Watch team are now being drawn up, but none of the essential large-scale separation measures is as yet even mooted. In their absence, the melancholy series of deaths is bound to continue.

Above *The Fire of Thine Eyes*
Below *Tara's three cubs at dinner*

13

THE MOMENT OF TRUTH

On September 28, 1980, as dusk was falling, a tiger was seen walking along the north bank of the Soheli, opposite Tiger Haven. It came to sit on the bank at Jungle Fowl Jetty, gazing over the water at the buildings, and it remained there after dark, evidently not worried by the powerful searchlight which I shone into its eyes. Only when Eelie started barking did it move away. In the beam of the lamp it looked a large animal, but investigation next morning revealed that it had been a tigress. I felt certain that this was Tara, returning to look at her old home.

Next night she came again. We did not see her, but tracks showed that she had approached from the east, this time along the south bank of the river, and passed directly in front of the servants' quarters lining the bank. Half-way along the row of garages adjoining the main hutments she turned right, between two of the buildings, crossed the river, and went to sit once more by the jetty, from where she presumably gazed at the place in which she had grown up.

A few evenings later a tigress again walked along the north bank of the river, and when I called to her with a *Prusten* – which had been my standard means of communication with Tara – she responded by spraying a tree three times, a sure sign of the tension my voice created. Then, as she moved on towards the jetty, I ran round the buildings, came back to the bank opposite her, and called her by name. This time she stopped, turned and for about thirty seconds looked at me as if in recollection of dim and far-off days. At last she moved slowly away.

I was both glad and sad that she had broken so completely with the past: glad, because by doing so she proved she was completely rehabilitated in the wild; and sad, because I was no longer able to share her life. Now I was also curious to know why she should come back and linger in her former haunts (an elderly lady to whom I related the episode remarked that her grown-up daughter behaved in exactly the same way!)

First I thought that Tara's visits might have been in search of food: as this was the end of the monsoon, we had no baits out, and it seemed that she might have come to look for one. Against this, she appeared well-fed, and on none of her three visits had she continued to the baiting site.

Another possible reason, I thought, might be that none of the male tigers with whom she had associated until recently had been a natural choice of mate. Old Crooked Foot was too old, and the other two – Tara's Male and Long Toes – too young and subordinate: in these circumstances I wondered whether a vague disquiet might perhaps have urged her to revisit old acquaintances. It was tantalising to understand so little of her motives.

Even so, this was the first time that I had had real confirmation that my former companion was alive and well, and I felt elated with a sense of achievement.

Towards the end of October, when we resumed baiting, Tara seemed to be associating mainly with Old Crooked Foot; but another visitor to the kills was the male I named the Young Tiger, son of the Big Tigress. The great question now was whether she would mate, and if so, with whom. She was then four and a half, and had not – as far as I knew – had any mating except the sterile one which took place when she was two and a half, and too young to conceive. I was beginning to worry, for everything I had read suggested that she should have had a fruitful mating before now. Tigresses in zoos often produce cubs at the age of three and a half or four – but of course conditions in the wild are entirely different. On the other hand both Schaller and Adamson, after a great deal of observation, agree that lionesses generally conceive between the ages of three and a half and four. Should not a wild tigress – a sister-species with a similar gestation period – be expected to breed on a similar schedule?

Towards the end of November Tara stopped coming to the baiting site, and the fact that she was seen with the Young Tiger near the Croc Bend, and with other males near the Dudhwa Barrier, made me hope that great events were about to take place. I therefore renovated the Narkul Machan overlooking the Twin Lakes grass-patch, and had a watcher sit up there until late in the evenings to check on any tell-tale sounds which might indicate that male and female were getting on with the job. The nights, however, remained obstinately silent, and Tara seemed to be avoiding both Old Crooked Foot and the Spillway baiting-site. Usually we found her pugs in the east, sometimes with those of Tara's Male sometimes with the Young Male's, but most often alone. On the one occasion when she did come to the Spillway site, she made no attempt to kill the bait.

On the night of January 16 from the Spillway Machan I heard a tremendous disturbance among the swamp deer, which began calling loudly soon after nine p.m. and went on until early morning. Tracking next day revealed that it was Tara who had been the cause of all the alarm: she had made a kill, and Old Crooked Foot, attracted by the calls, had left his own kill at the Spillway site to go and join her at it. The Young Tiger had also fed on the swamp deer – as we could tell from the hair in a dropping which he later deposited on the Leopard Bridge.

In early February Tara once more began to frequent the Spillway site, often leaving her spray on her favourite jamun tree, but she seemed to avoid the kill-site itself. The key question now was whether or not she had mated, unknown to me, during the peak period which had just passed. There had been certain behavioural changes – she had pointedly aban-doned the company of Old Crooked Foot, and had begun associating with the daughter of the Median Tigress – but this was hardly positive evidence. Then, on the night of February 24, Old Crooked Foot abruptly abandoned the range after a two-year reign: he moved away overnight, and Tara's Male took over.

He was young and vigorous, and well able to kill mature buffaloes, but his skill in this respect was not much use to Tara for the moment, as she seemed to make a point of avoiding him. In any case, he was only partially dependent on the baits, and would disappear westwards for long intervals on hunting expeditions of his own. This left her to tackle baits as best she could – and at that stage she was not very effective.

Apparently nervous of tackling full-grown buffaloes, she evolved a technique of her own for dealing with them. To avoid the necessity of a throat-attack, she would stalk the bait while it was lying down and then leap on it to prevent it getting to its feet, mauling and biting its hindquarters until it was incapacitated.

This method was much more cruel than the normal killing-process of a tiger. Also, Tara was very wasteful with a large kill, as she would feed on it for only two days before abandoning it.

To overcome these problems I resolved to create a separate baiting site, especially for Tara, and to use small buffaloes, or paddas (buffalo calves), which she would be able to kill cleanly. The danger, of course, was that if her male discovered the site he would make short work of the small baits, and leave not even a snack for Tara; but that was a risk I had to accept.

Since Tara usually went off eastwards after her visits to the baiting-site, I made plans to intercept her along her regular route, harrowing a roadway from the Haldu Machan to the Madrahia road, and cutting a pathway from under a small ficus tree to a pool in the river. (Tigers use footpaths for preference, chiefly because of the quietness, good visibility and freedom from obstructions which they offer.) Finally I put up a machan in the ficus. I was delighted to find that on her next visit Tara had walked along the new road. Waiting until the male had gone off on one of his prolonged excursions, after finishing a kill, I tied up a small bait at the new site, and on the second night Tara killed it with a nape-grip. (This seemed to confirm that her cruel method of dealing with the large buffaloes was designed to make sure that she did not get injured.)

Encouraged by the success of my strategy, I decided to spend the next night on the machan, armed with a camera and remote-control apparatus, so that I could get close-up pictures. So far everything had worked perfectly, but now trouble set in. Before I went to the machan I test-fired the camera, and it worked perfectly; but at night, when I heard Tara on the kill and pushed the firing-button, nothing happened.

The sound of Tara's contented chomping should have been music to my ears, but in spite of it I was consumed with irritation. For some time I sat watching the sterile spark flickering from the remote-control receiver; then I could stand the suspense no longer, and shone a searchlight on the bait. As Tara moved off I got down and disconnected the motor drive before walking home disconsolately. Evidently Tara was not unduly alarmed by these extraordinary proceedings, for she returned and ate a good deal more of the kill. On the third night she removed the head and cracked the cranium to scoop out the brains – something I had never known a tiger do before. The next night I put Jackson on the machan with instructions on how to operate the camera, but his luck was no better than mine: hearing an animal on the kill, he fired off, only to find that the nocturnal visitor was Tiffany, my fishing cat, who had come to indulge in a spot of scavenging.

Still I was determined to get close-up pictures, and so I soon resolved to spend another night on the machan. The moon was bright, and at about 11 p.m. I watched the bait, a buffalo calf, unconcernedly chewing its cud. Suddenly there was a groan and a brittle snap as the animal's vertebrae were crushed. Tara had seized it with a nape-grip and killed in under a minute.

This time the camera worked perfectly. I got six pictures, but the flashes alarmed Tara enough to prevent her returning that night. Next night I left her in peace: she ate a good deal, and I heard her calling as she went off towards Chorleekh. The third night she returned once more, and again opened the brain-pan. Whereas she had at one time avoided buffalo kills, she now appeared to have become hooked on baiting, possibly because the paddas were more tender and tasted better, and would visit the site every second day.

Her special site was only about 400 yards from the old one, and it was clear that her preferential treatment could not last.

Sure enough, the male returned unexpectedly from a long-range patrol, found the new site and demolished the small bait in short order. Thereafter tracks showed that he and Tara began to consort with each other a good deal. My hopes of a mating rose again, and, on the supposition that the two tigers would share kills from now on, I reverted to baiting with large buffaloes at the old site.

By now Tara was approaching her fifth birthday, and as I felt certain she was not pregnant, I hoped more than ever that she would soon mate. At least she had begun going round with a male again; also, she was calling quite frequently, which I took to be a good sign.

On May 5 – her birthday – we put out a well-grown bait and, although she did not come, the male arrived at 1.30 a.m. and killed the buffalo with a nape-grip. In the morning I was surprised to find that he had not fed. If a tiger has had a severe struggle to subdue a victim, it often does not feed immediately; but in this case there had scarcely been a struggle at all. The male, full of confidence, had killed the buffalo in classic tiger fashion in thirty seconds. The explanation of this apparent anomaly came next night: rather than feeding, the male had gone off to fetch his tigress, and now they both dragged the kill of into the dense bushes north-west of the Spillway.

Next morning, May 7, a miracle occurred: at last I had the rare privilege of being able to watch wild tigers mating – and of being present, moreover, at the nuptials of the tigress with whom I had been so closely connected.

Early in the morning I crept silently to the River Bend hide, and from it, on a sandspit opposite the Leopard Haven spillway, I saw the bulky form of the male lying down. Through my binoculars I also made out the slimmer shape of Tara reclining beside him under the shade of some jamun trees. After a while she got up, walked to the edge of the water, and crouched with her tail to one side, clearly in invitation, keeping up a hollow, vibrant growling as a sign of her receptive condition. The male promptly rose and mounted her, but no sooner had he taken the nape of her neck in a symbolic grip then she whirled round on him with an explosive snarl, and he hastily backed off.

After this preliminary attempt at copulation, Tara lay on her back with her paws in the air, while the male went sedately back to his old position. Soon, however, she got up again and walked over to him. Then she tantalised him by brushing provocatively against his head, flicking his nose with her tail, and presenting her hindquarters in front of him. When there was no immediate response, she seemed to become even more restless, and walked into the river. The tiger followed, with a bemused expression on his face, and as he passed her she rubbed her head against his, before rubbing her entire sinuous body against his bulk. So far all the preliminary, flirtatious advances had been hers.

The pair were not so besotted that they failed to notice Mira, my sister-in-law, as she slipped into the hide to join me. First Tara, and then the tiger, moved off into the bushes. In the evening their calls sounded from further west, so I got Jackson and some other labourers to continue clearing a pathway beyond the hide to a high point overlooking the river opposite Leopard Haven which I called the White Cliffs, for the carpet of dry leaves crackled noisily when one walked and made stealthy approaches impossible.

Next morning the tigers were in the thick cover directly north of Leopard Haven: though I could not at first see them, I could tell exactly where they were from the nasal moan of the male and the answering growls of the female. At 9.20 a.m. the sounds ceased, as they no doubt cat-napped, recovering from their nocturnal labours, but an hour later they appeared in the water beneath the escarpment, where Prince used to play with Eelie.

I watched them spellbound from behind a termite hill, but Jackson unfortunately was still working on the path-clearance, and the tigress's acute ears picked up a faint crackling as he came towards me. Tara moved back into cover, but her mate was too comfortable and too confident to shift. He sat on in the water, and with soft, moaning grunts summoned his tigress back. Soon she appeared on the bank and presented, whereupon he got out of the water and mounted her. With each powerful thrust his nasal moan increased in volume and vibrated like a dynamo, until at the climax she turned on him with an explosive roar and his tail shot up in the air as he hastened to dismount. Tara then lay on her back, and later moved into the water with him. Soon after that they went back under cover, and the sounds of their courtship continued unabated.

The following morning – the third day – they were still *in situ*. Except for a period of respite similar to that of the day before, their calls continued. Tara's hollow, vibrant growling seemed even louder: it was such a strange, mechanical sound that when Mira heard it she said 'What on earth's that?' and thought that a motor-boat was coming up the river. It seemed to me that, if anything, the male's desire had strengthened since the series of matings began, and now he was going full throttle.

So it continued all that day and into the night, which proved to be the last: next morning the tigers had gone their separate ways, and when I walked out to Leopard Haven I found that during the night Tara had crossed the river and come past the termite hill from which I had watched her. So ended three of the most fascinating and rewarding days I have ever spent in the jungle.

A few days later, as I was walking along the north bank of the river, I saw Tara drinking water opposite the Double-Storey Machan. Waiting until she was about to pass me, only twenty yards off, I called to her. She turned her face, and the look of semi-acknowledgement that I knew so well came over her expression as she gazed at me. She watched me for nearly thirty seconds before slowly cantering up the escarpment.

Knowing that she would cross the Am Danda to go east, I hurried on there, and when she emerged on to the road, some 200 yards away, I called to her again as I watched through binoculars. Once more she wore the look of dawning recognition, not quite complete. I wondered what the circumstances of our meeting would have to be to impel her to take one step in my direction!

I was thrilled to have seen her, and to have been half-recognised. The day had one more treat in store for me. In the evening we went for a drive, and just beyond the Neora Bridge in the Neora–Nagrol catchment area a large leopard crossed the road. He crouched under cover, and it was not until I drove the Jeep within five yards of him that he broke out and ran. This had been Prince's favourite habitat; at that date he would have been ten years old; and since the area contained so few leopards, I reckoned this could well have been my former companion. The sighting brought a red-letter day to a perfect end.

Quite by chance, the excitement of Tara's mating had hardly died down when we found ourselves in the middle of another nuptial circus. At 2 p.m. on June 1, about twenty days after Tara's mating, the Median Tigress's daughter, who had come into season, began to call loudly from the region of the Monsoon Machan. At the time Jackson happened to be watching Tara and her male, who were both sitting in the river opposite the Western Spillway. At each call they jerked to attention, but otherwise took no action, remaining where they were in the cool stream.

The calling continued intermittently until the early night, when it took on a greater urgency. Next night the Chief Wildlife Warden saw a pair of tigers on the escarpment above the Leopard Bridge, and later their mating roars continued in the area of Juliette Point. Theirs, it seemed, was a movable feast. The following night the male arrived at the Spillway site in the company of both Tara and the Median's daughter, and he mated frequently with the latter near the Haldu Machan.

Since I knew that the young tigress was only two years and nine months old, I assumed she was having the same kind of abortive mating that Tara had gone through at a similar age: two smears of vaginal blood certainly pointed to her juvenile status. (Harriet had also mated at about the same age, and gone through some form of phantom pregnancy.) In any case, the pair spent the next day to the west of the farm, between the Spillway site and Leopard Haven, but we heard no calls except one snarl from the kill-site. Thereafter they came into the water, but not for long. Late in the evening the tigress began calling again, now opposite Leopard Haven, and then set off rapidly along the escarpment as far as the Twin Lakes, calling as she went. That night, however, the pair were back in the west. The following evening she travelled east once more, again calling loudly, this time to the south of the farm. The restless mating, and frequent calling by the tigress, continued until the night of June 6, when the pair at last separated. The tigress then joined the Young Tiger, and after a spot of communal rolling the two set off towards the Pallia Road.

This series of matings was quite different from the static session of three days and three nights which appears to be normal among tigers and leopards: it was remarkable for the restlessness and continuous calling of the tigress. These, I believe, were due to the presence of a resident tigress (Tara), and the absence of any preliminary courtship – two factors which prolonged the mating-time to a week. Another point of interest was that the vaginal smear was not deposited until the second night of mating. This suggested to me that the initial bouts of copulation between the big cats may be symbolic, rather than fully consummated, and that they are an essential part of courtship, without which the volatile reactions of the mating partners might lead to serious injury.

Once the series of matings were over, the tigers re-paired themselves: the male returned to the company of Tara, whereas the Median's daughter went off with the Young Tiger; and it struck me that the solitary status of the tiger may well be due more to constrictions imposed by the lack of prey than to any obsessive desire to be alone.

14

THE FIRE OF THINE EYES

In May 1981 a significant incident took place in the grassland between Tiger Haven and the main Pallia-Dudhwa road. The Young Tiger – son of the Big Tigress – now spent much of his time in this area, where the pre-monsoon showers had quickened the growth of lush grasses in low-lying spots. The new cover not only provided tigers with good habitat, but also furnished them with a temporary increase of prey in the form of the domestic stock which accompanied the buffalo carts and their owners when they came to cut fodder.

Here, one day, the Young Tiger charged out at a buffalo conveniently tethered to a cart on the edge of a grass patch. At that very second Chamkaur Singh, the cart-owner, happened to appear, dead on the tiger's line, between him and his target. Instead of carrying on and knocking the man down, the tiger veered off sharply and disappeared back into the cover: even in the excitement of an attack he had deliberately avoided a human being.

Politicians and sycophantic bureaucrats had been continually asserting that the tigers of Kheri had all become compulsive man-eaters; but here was proof positive that man was *not* normally regarded as a prey species, even in a place where the tigers had grown used to the presence of humans. The incident also demonstrated that humans were constantly violating tiger habitat, which the law forbade them to enter, and confirmed my contention that the only safe insurance against conflict between man and tiger would be an effectively-enforced no-man's land between the two sides.

The Young Tiger, deprived of his victim on that occasion, went on to kill a bony scrub-cow in a thorn patch next to the Nakauwha, where he was later joined by Tara and her male. A few more cattle were killed before the scene was once again transformed by the advent of the main monsoon, when floods and cattle flies drove the domestic herds towards their homes and the tigers to higher ground on top of the escarpment. There would now, I knew, be a temporary truce until the return of drier weather once more gave the human scavengers access to the forest.

Normally I used to stop baiting during the rainy season; but because Tara had mated two months ago, and would probably now be carrying her first set of cubs, I resolved to go on feeding her, to help her during pregnancy and while she was rearing the family. Unlike a lion, whose pride-mates would help out in such circumstances, she would have to depend mainly on her own capabilities, and, as she would be handicapped, I felt it my duty to assist her, not only as an extension of my pilot experiment in rehabilitation, but for sentimental reasons as well. I was not making an attempt to get her back. Far from it: she had lived as a wild tigress for over three years now, and there was no question of her becoming dependent on my help, but even so I thought I would tide her over a difficult time of her life.

I was still being heavily criticised in some quarters for my practice of regular baiting, and among the critics there were two schools of thought. First, there were the sentimentalists, who maintained that the practice was cruel, as the tied-up bait has no chance of escape. To this the obvious answer is that neither does a battery-reared bird or animal, or even a normally-reared animal which goes to a butcher.

The other school – the so-called experts – claimed that baiting was not only against the Indian national philosophy, but also counter-productive: tigers got so used to tethered baits (the argument ran) that they lost their natural killing technique, and, if baiting was stopped, took to the easiest alternative form of prey – man. My own experience of nearly twenty-five years' regular baiting leads me to reject these arguments as utterly spurious. I have already (in Chapter 4) described the horrors of Muhammadan butchers and Khatik pig-killers, and explained why I think it in every way preferable for an animal to die in the jungle, rather than in a primitive slaughter-yard. Yet, quite apart from the issue of possible cruelty, there are many moral and practical considerations in favour of baiting.

Now that we have so devastated our wildlife and its habitat, we cannot let a doctrine of *laissez-faire* take the place of positive wildlife management. No longer can we apply principles which were adequate when our virgin forests still covered half the country. Rather, we must take active, practical measures to help the great cats survive, particularly in times of stress. Nowhere in India are wildlife populations other than subnormal, and it is only commonsense to take some of the pressure off them by sacrificing surplus domestic animals, which would otherwise die of maltreatment or starvation. To disallow this practice, as the Forest Department does, shows an extraordinarily regressive attitude on the part of the organisation which is supposed to look after wildlife.

It is equally unrealistic to claim that regular baiting deprives tigers of their natural killing ability. Although they are said by some people to have no taste glands, I have found that they do have definite food-preferences, and buffaloes – the normal bait – come low on their list of priorities. I have often found that healthy, full-grown tigers bypass tethered buffaloes at close range and go off hunting wild prey. Their inherited instincts are so strong that they will never allow their killing expertise, on which survival depends, to become atrophied. Finally, the claim that tigers who get used to easy prey progress to man-eating is an absolutely baseless charge, unworthy of the Forest Department whose job is to protect our national animal. There is simply no connection between baiting and man-eating: as I have repeatedly said, humans are not a natural prey species for tigers, and it is only in adverse conditions specifically created by the master race that man-eating begins.

To return to my story: as usual during the monsoon, the Spillway site was flooded, and as I wanted to help Tara, rather than the local tigers in general, I had somehow to keep baits concealed from the male who was quite capable of looking after himself. I therefore tried tethering a buffalo calf about 100 yards east of Tiger Haven, at a point which Tara sometimes used to pass after her tour of the southern circuit. Unfortunately the male heard the calf calling as it was tied up, and took it away across the river, where he finished it at a sitting. Thus I needed to find a new site, and I chose the spot where the Am Danda came down the escarpment to the Leopard Bridge.

Towards the end of July a well-grown bait was killed there by the Median's Daughter, and shared between her and Tara, who fed on alternate nights. The next bait – a smaller one – was killed with a side-grip by Tara, who pulled it away some 300 yards to the north-west, where she ate it with evident appreciation. In the morning, when Jackson and I followed up the drag, she was lying close by the remains: we saw the bushes quiver as we reached the spot where the remnants were tucked away in a patch of dense undergrowth. It had been raining, and as we went on and emerged on to the Sathiana road we glimpsed her sitting in a pool of water. She moved hastily back into cover with a growl, and I quickly slipped a lead on to Eelie, who had been following the trail with us.

That night both tigresses finished off the kill. But I feared it was not going to be possible to conceal their activities from Tara's Male for long, and after a couple of abortive visits to the baiting-site during the afternoon he came along on the night of August 14 and made a kill of his own. I saw that I would not be able to hoodwink him any more, and accepted the fact that the site would have to be a communal one.

By then I reckoned that Tara's pregnancy must be almost at full term. I knew that zoo records put the normal length of a tiger pregnancy at 105 days, but I also knew that it could vary, especially with a first family. Tara and her male had parted company on the night of May 9; the 105th day after that was August 21, and as that approached, I watched hopefully for some sudden change in Tara's behaviour or routine which would tell me that the cubs had been born, and so determine the exact length of a wild tigress's delivery period.

I had reckoned, however, without the highly secretive nature of a wild tigress; and even though I had seen Harriet, my she-leopard perform the extraordinary feat of climbing seventy feet up a vertical tree-trunk only an hour before she gave birth, I had not fully appreciated the way in which Nature has made arrangements to deprive a solitary predator of her capabilities for the shortest possible time. Thus I noticed no change in Tara's routine, beyond the fact that she spent the 23rd and the 24th – the 107th and 108th days – in a ravine behind Prince's Monsoon Machan. I suspected that she might have had the cubs there, but I did not want to risk disturbing her by going to look, and there was no definite sign that they had arrived.

By then I had shifted the kill-site to a spot across the river from the Double-Storey Machan, where a nice, deep ravine ran back into the escarpment. Tara became a regular visitor, and made most of the kills herself, even though other tigers shared them with her. She now despatched full-grown buffaloes with the regulation neck-grip, and it was clear that at the age of five she had grown into a mature tigress, with an added confidence which seemed to have come with her pregnancy. After feeding she would come to the river bank and spend a great deal of time sitting in the soft mud before departing up the ravine.

Not until September 4 – the 118th day – did she give a sure sign that her pregnancy was over. Then she broke her normal routine by going off westwards to a ravine opposite the Western Spillway, and during the short journey she sprayed ten times, marking the way to the spot to which – I suspected – she had now shifted the cubs: for security reasons, the great cats do not keep their young in any one place for long.

At that point, unfortunately, I had to go to London, and I was away about six weeks; on my return Jackson had nothing special to report. He had not seen any cubs, and although Tara was about, her visits to the kill-site had fallen off. As if to inform me that all was well, she called fourteen times from the west on October 24, just after I had got back: I took these for warning calls, and assumed from them that she and her cubs were still headquartered in that locality.

I now tried to take some flashlight photographs at the kill-site, and for some time I was puzzled by the fact that although the tigers came to feed when the equipment was not set up, they would not come when it was. Only after much frustration did I realise that the battery recycled itself with a faint squeak which, though hardly audible to human ears, was enough to put the tigers off.

One morning at daybreak a flurry of chital alarm-calls came from the river junction just upstream of Tiger Haven, and Tara swam the river holding a female chital in her jaws. She went up the escarpment, crossed the old kill-site, and took her prize off along the drag-route which she had earlier used for removing young buffaloes. Evidently she heard us following up her line, for when we found the carcass, she had left it, having eaten very little. We pulled it to the kill-site, in the hope that we might thus get a photograph of her, but although she was particularly partial to chital, she was wary enough of the intrusion not to return, and the carcass was sadly allowed to rot.

Soon after this the Median's Daughter visited the site and attacked a fairly large buffalo. Still being amateurish in her killing-methods, she was ·nable to subdue it, and abandoned it with a longitudinal scrat.h down its back. Such is the poison carried in a tiger's retractile claws (generated by contact with putrefying flesh) that although the scratch was a comparatively minor one, and we bathed it with a disinfectant, the animal swelled up immediately and died within three days, its flesh soon turning green thereafter!

One highlight of the New Year was Tara's capture of a swamp deer stag. Having heard a great deal of calling from the deer in the grass south-east of Leopard Haven, I went to investigate and found her pug-marks leading into a patch of tall grass. Following up Tara's trail, I came on the remains of a swamp deer stag with a fine fourteen-point head. The animal must have weighed between 400 and 500 lbs, and I knew that her prey-range had reached the maximum possible.

All this time, I need hardly say, we had been hoping to see

the cubs; and it gives some idea of their mother's wariness, as well as of the jungle's density – that we found no trace of them until early February, when they were five months old. Then one morning I saw the pug-marks of a tigress who had walked down into a ravine opposite Leopard Haven. Close by it was the single track of what I casually took to be a leopard, and I was pleased to think that some progeny of Prince must be wandering around. A few days later, however, on the road from Madrahia, close to the swamp deer kill, I again came on the tracks of a tigress, and this time, embedded in the slush left by heavy overnight rain, were the paw-marks of two cubs.

My heart leapt at the sight – the first proof that the cubs were alive. They had splashed along through the puddles in deep wheel-marks like young human children and then pushed their way into the grass. It was a thrilling discovery. Although I had found it hard to believe that such a purposeful mating sequence as I had seen could have been unsuccessful, I had not dared to hope too much, especially as I had read in Schaller's book *The Deer and the Tiger* that among one group of captive lions only 38 per cent of matings had been productive. Now I knew for sure that Tara had produced a truly wild family.

Next day I came on their pug-marks going up a ravine opposite the Western Spillway, and on the lip of the escarpment we found a few bones and some hair of a chital, which they appeared to have demolished completely. Eelie grew very alarmed – the spot must have reeked of tigers to her – but although it looked as if the family was living in the area, we saw no more signs of them. A picture which I took of Tara in early February showed she was still suckling then, but I think she must have weaned the cubs soon after that (they are normally weaned at about five months).

Tara was apparently now confident that she could safely introduce her family to the other tigers of the range, for she began bringing them to kills, where a male, two females and the cubs all shared the same carcasses – subject, of course, to prevailing protocol. The cubs seemed to gnaw at rib-ends and the rump, but did not actually eat very much, and the circumstantial evidence again strengthened my belief that a mother may regurgitate half-digested meat for her offspring until they are big enough to join in communal hunts at the age of about nine months.

By the middle of February they had become regular visitors, and one morning, having inspected the kill, I walked on to a hide overlooking a sand-spit on which crocodiles sometimes bask. As I crept cautiously towards the blind I trod on a dead leaf, which crackled faintly, and at once I heard low growls start up on the far bank of the river. At first I thought that Tara was threatening the male, who had been on the kill with her, but when I peered through a hole in the blind I found she was looking straight at it, her suspicions alerted by the slight sound that I had made. Suddenly two cubs walked out on to the sand, but they were immediately subdued by their mother's growling and moved away, with her following – an impressive illustration of how she shielded them from danger.

Some fifteen days after our first sighting of the two cubs, we found the pugs of a third. Already I had spent many nights out in the hope of seeing the family, and now I went up the Double-Storey Machan for yet another stint of waiting. This time, at least, I was quickly rewarded: soon after dark there was a noise in the dry leaves like a herd of elephants approaching, as the cubs rushed helter-skelter to the kill. Luckily there was bright moonlight, and I could see them clearly as they wandered round while their mother and father ate.

Having fed, the family moved a little way up the river and disported themselves on the bank. Now and then I could see them on a large patch of white sand which had built up on a bend, but I knew they were there all night from the intermittent splashing that kept breaking out.

At first light silence reigned, so I climbed down off the machan with the intention of relieving myself before crossing the river on an enormous sal trunk which had fallen across the stream and served as a bridge for tigers and humans alike. Just as I was about to step off the bank there was a sudden scurry, and two cubs rushed into view, chasing each other, within ten yards of where I was standing. Both parties stared at each other, the cubs sitting on their hunkers with expressions of amazement on their little faces at finding they were not alone on the sandbank. Abruptly it struck me that their mother could not be far away, and that she would not be at all pleased if she found me so close to her offspring. I therefore withdrew stealthily and went back up the machan, all desire to answer the call of nature having vanished in the excitement of meeting the cubs at such close quarters. They too beat a furtive retreat, into the grass from which they had erupted.

For a few more minutes I sat on the machan, glowing with pleasure as I waited for Jackson to arrive, which he did fairly soon. Then, having armed myself with a heavy stick, which I often carry as a psychological rather than a physical deterrent, I wrapped a scarf round my neck against the chill dawn air and set off to cross the log bridge. Its corrugated surface was treacherous to our shoes wet with dew, so we had to pick our way across with care. In some places the bridge was covered with wet sand, and this was indented with pug-marks of both mother and cubs, showing where they had crossed and re-crossed several times in the night.

As the river bend came into view I again began to hear splashes to my left, and I crept forward to the upturned root of a great tree which towered above my head, its slender end-tentacles waving gently in the breeze. From that vantage point I beheld an enchanting sight – all three cubs, playing in the river. Two sat solemnly in the water, immersed up to their small heads, while the third kept scrambling on to a horizontal log, whence it would leap back into the stream. No wonder I had heard splashes during the night! I could imagine the tight-shut eyes as the cub screwed up its courage before launching off into the rippling current below.

Now, as I watched fascinated, a movement farther up the river caught my eye. There on the bank sat the mother, anxiously watching her offspring from a patch of bracken. Soon, inevitably, she caught sight of us and stood up to roar defiance at the intruders on the family scene. Explosive bursts of noise echoed through the tall trees. At once the gambolling cubs knew that something was wrong and scampered off into the jungle, water spraying from their coats. I would have given anything to have had a movie-camera at that moment.

It so happened that this was the very river bend on which I had called to Tara a year ago, when she had looked at me with recognition before moving away. Now her circumstances had changed: there was no recognition in her eyes, only a burning concern for the safety of her cubs. Moreover, she appeared to have been considerably alarmed by this encounter, for the family vanished after it, and not until a fortnight later did I find their returning pugs about a mile away.

With the weather again getting warmer, I resolved to shift the baiting-site back to the Spillway Machan, which was more secluded and thus a more likely place for the tigers to cool off. One morning at first light I went to check the bait, and as I crept slowly up the ladder to the machan I thought I heard a faint growl. When I looked through the screen, I saw Tara standing next to the dead buffalo, growling softly, with her gaze fixed on the machan. Through my binoculars I had a wonderful view of her: with absolute clarity I made out the inverted catapult of stripes on her left cheek, her characteristic eye-spot. I thought she had never looked so beautiful.

I was seized by an almost-overwhelming desire to go and stroke her; to tell her that I wished her family no harm; to say that although she had left me for her own kind and a better world, I still loved her and wished her well. But she, indifferent to my telepathic messages, soon moved off and sat down beyond the Spillway, where a cub came and massaged its back against her chin.

After such a morning I felt bound to spend yet another night on the machan – and again I saw some action. Two cubs came to the kill soon after dark, and proceeded to gnaw at it. Then, around midnight, I heard the third sibling call from across the river, where – I presumed – it was waiting with Tara. It seemed likely that this third member of the family, who had appeared on the scene much later than the other two, was the weakest and most backward, and even when Tara came to the kill just before daybreak, it did not accompany her. The mother sensed that the machan was occupied, and led her family away before it got light, giving off menacing growls all the time.

When the hot weather really set in, I expected we should start seeing tigers in the river regularly, and indeed one day I found Tara's Male sitting in the water opposite the Western Spillway. Jackson therefore put up a low machan commanding this site, and after the next kill (made by Tara herself) I climbed up to spend the day on it. I was expecting a friend of mine in the Forest Department, whom I had invited to come and take pictures of Tara; a virulent campaign was then raging, as my enemies tried to establish that she had been shot as a man-eater, and I wanted someone connected with the Department to get pictures that would settle the argument. When the man arrived, I sent him off with Jackson to occupy the River Bend hide, as I thought that would give him the best chance.

My own machan faced westwards, up the river, and gave a good view in that direction. The trouble with it was that the south side, on my left, was not properly screened, and as I sat there I was exposed to any animal that might come along the far bank of the river.

Needless to say, that was where the tigers appeared. Not long after my friend had gone a monkey coughed once, and a cub appeared on the south bank. Hardly had I brought my binoculars to bear on it when there was a violent explosion of rage as Tara caught the movement of the glasses and strode purposefully along the bank towards me. Roar after roar resounded through the forest. Once she paused at a gap in the tall grass, and I saw her furious face glaring at me. She continued her advance until she was right opposite me, only twenty yards away, and then she came on to sit in the water, whence she continued to growl and snarl at me, clearly saying that if I intended to threaten her young family, I would have to try conclusions with her first!

The cubs, meanwhile, had come down the Central Spillway and begun to play in the water right underneath my sister-in-law Mira, who was sitting high in a jamun tree. (According to her, one of them was definitely weaker than the other two, and this seemed to confirm the theory that the last of a family may sometimes not be strong enough to survive.) After a while Tara seemed to think she had admonished me enough: her expression gradually changed from one of defensive threat to one of indifference and she returned to lead her offspring into some grass on the opposite bank, from which she gave a series of sambar-like *pooks* – a call which seems designed to communicate a mixture of alarm and suspicion, and which I had heard repeated several times one night when Tara was approaching a kill with the cubs.

The only watchers who saw no tigers that day were Jackson and my friend who, poor man, had had the alarming experience of hearing the full-throated roars of an invisible tiger gradually drawing closer to the hide in which he was perched; and when, later, he realised that on his way back he had passed close by the grass patch in which the tiger family had taken cover, he seriously warned me to be more careful in future!

As the cubs became more independent, they began to visit kills on their own. Once they came to inspect the baiting-site during the day, and I liked to think that in the evening they led their mother to the place where she could provide them with a meal that night.

Next morning, attracted by the alarm-cough of a langur, I crept into the River Bend Hide at about nine a.m., and found what I took to be a smallish tiger lying below me on the sand, behind a washed-out tree-root. At first I thought it was one of the cubs, but then I realised that its fur was short, and more clean-cut-looking than the thick coats of the cubs. Moreover, I was looking down, which does make an animal seem smaller than it is. As soon as the creature shifted position, I realised it was Tara herself.

The hide was on an exposed piece of ground; and, with the sun beating down on me, and the clay hard under my backside, I began to grow restive, irrationally feeling irritated with the tigress for lying at her ease on the cool sand and not producing activity enough to justify the use of any film. Nor was there any sign of the cubs. But I decided to skip lunch and wait for them, and at last, about 4.30 p.m. one of them appeared from the Spillway, walking along the bank, only to take a brief dip and disappear back into cover. A short while later a second cub came out. This one too had a dip, and then lay down within ten yards of its mother.

By then it was five o'clock, and after spending some eight hours in the company of my former companion, without food or water on a scorching May day, I had a splitting headache. Since neither Tara nor the cub showed any sign of moving, I coughed to get some action. Instantly the tigress sat up and accurately pin-pointed the source of the alien sound. A moment later she began to snarl and growl, whereupon the cub got the message and moved quickly into the jungle. Tara herself immediately went and sat down symbolically on the spot the cub had just vacated, demonstrating that she intended to protect it, and from there she continued to threaten her unseen watcher. As for me, I crept away feeling that all those hours of discomfort had been infinitely well worthwhile, just to get that one glimpse of a mother's watchfulness and concern.

Sometimes, however, I did not have to wait interminably in baking hides for a worthwhile sighting. One afternoon in mid-May I walked along the north bank of the river, sweat pouring down my back in rivulets, and climbed up to the machan from which I had watched Tara roaring defiance at me a few days before. Three-quarters of the way up the ladder, through a chink in the camouflage, I caught sight of the tigress sitting in the water. Already she had detected some faint sound that I must have made: there was a tense expression on her face as she tried to locate it. Next to her, in a tight little circle, sat the three cubs, only their small heads showing, looking for all the world as if they were debating some abstruse situation. Although at first they appeared secure in the confidence that their mother's presence gave them, after about ten minutes they responded to some indistinguishable signal from her and moved into cover. Soon after, as I climbed down the ladder, she followed them.

By the time the cubs were ten months old I assumed that they had started to accompany and help their mother on hunting expeditions, for it is at about this age that young tigers usually begin learning to earn their living. One sign of increasing independence was the way in which they came to Tara's kills by themselves. Then, during early June, visits to the baiting-site eased off, and instead there was a great deal of calling by hog deer in the grasslands south and east of Tiger Haven. The cubs' pug-marks were seen in the east near Tara's Crossing, and it now seemed possible that they were hunting on their own.

A few days later I found Tara in her favourite spot on the sandbank near the River Bend Hide. Two cubs were with her, but soon they got up and ambled into the forest. Although she stayed where she was for a while, she seemed concerned and kept raising her head to look around. Suddenly she got up and walked purposefully into the jungle on the trail left by the family, but just as I was wondering why she had departed, she returned and lay down again in her original position. Clearly she had gone to check on the cubs, for after a few moments first one and then the other came out into the water, one lying down next to her while the other wandered about in the stream.

Each day that went by made me more anxious about the third sibling, and I could not help fearing that the runt had succumbed to life's pressures, in spite of my efforts to succour the whole family. Jackson reassured me by saying that he had recently found a set of three different tracks, all together, and there was also the possibility that, if the third cub was a male, it had already started staying away from its sisters in a demonstration of independence. For the moment the mystery remained unresolved.

Over a month later the family still had not been back to the Spillway site, and as alarm-calls continued to resound from the east, I staked a bait out there, praying that Tara's Male would not put in an appearance. He had not passed that way for a considerable time, but now, with the perversity of his race, he came and took the bait and fed mightily for two nights. By the time Tara and her family arrived, on the third night, there was precious little left.

Late next evening I at last got a good view of the third cub, which I found sitting on a patch of wet sand in the river bed. I could see now that she was a female, and to my anxious eyes she looked ill. When she got up and headed for the bank, she moved hesitantly, and her hindquarters (the touchstone of health in a cat) looked weak, with the hip-bones sticking up prominently. My heart went out to the spindly little creature: she was often absent from the kill-site, and several of my photographs showed her sitting around while the others gorged themselves. I would have worried about her less if I had known what effort the mother was making to look after her.

That same evening before sunset Tara and the two stronger cubs pulled down a cow grazing to the east of the Pallia road. As if to make certain that there would be enough food to go round,

she also killed a bullock about a hundred yards away, presumably leaving the cubs at the first kill – for minor scratches
showed that they had joined in the attack. Then she went off in
search of the weakling, and led it to the kill as well. When I saw
what she had done I felt deeply touched by her maternal
solicitude, so much in contrast with the behaviour of the social
lioness, which does not hesitate to abandon subnormal cubs to
their fate; and I determined to help the family over this difficult
time when the mother would have to kill enough to feed three
ever-more-hungry young.

It was no help that both the cow and the bullock had been
killed in the open. Tara's Male came and pulled the bullock
away a bit, but then vultures spotted both carcasses and
descended to clean up the remains: within ten minutes a swarm
of them had devoured everything except the bones. I therefore
put out another bait, which Tara killed in the early part of the
night. After she had fed I heard her calling the cubs to join her,
and they did so one night later.

The monsoon was late that year: by early July the river had
risen very little, and one morning the men who went to put out
a bait reported that the weakling cub was lying out on a patch of
sand. I went to have a look, and found the little tigress stretched
out on the water's edge. She looked even worse than before.
Now and then she sat up to glance round, before rolling over on
to her other side, but her brown eyes appeared sunken and
lustreless. I left her lying where she was, for I had begun to
suspect that she had some other ailment besides hunger; but I
also hoped that if Tara came and killed the bait, which was only
about 200 yards away, the weakling might join her at it and get
a square meal.

That night there was rain, and although Tara did kill the
buffalo early on, her calls to the cubs brought no response. I
thought that the two bigger ones might have gone to look for
pickings at the old cow-kill, but I feared the worst for their
sister.

Next day, however, I was greatly relieved to find that she was
still alive. Early in the afternoon the male appeared – perhaps
after hearing Tara's calls to her cubs in the night – and dragged
the kill off into some tall grass. Two hours later the weakling

emerged and sat down in the shade of an acacia tree. For two hours she lay there listlessly, and then she walked very slowly to the empty kill-site. She looked pathetic: her hip-bones stuck out on either side of her backbone, and her mouth hung open as she nosed along the trail left by the carcass as her father dragged it. After a drink of water from a mudhole, she continued slowly along the drag. Slow as she was, she followed the trail with scarcely any hesitation, and when she momentarily went wrong where he had entered the tall grass, she quickly corrected her mistake and disappeared from sight. It was remarkable to watch such a diminutive and wretched figure carefully following the scent trail and confidently entering the forbidding undergrowth into which the great tiger had taken his dinner a few hours earlier – and I felt like shouting a warning. By the next morning the entire family had zeroed in on the kill, and there was nothing left of a 300–400 lb animal except a heap of bones. I felt unreasonably irritated with the big fellow for eating so much of the family's food, even though I had to concede that all tigers function on the basis of quid pro quo.

Following this feast, the weak cub recovered with extra-ordinary speed, as they do at that age. After the next kill, a few days later, all three youngsters came to feed in the middle of the day, and the weakling, looking much less feeble, pulled so mightily at a piece of gristle that when it snapped she fell over backwards. The biggest cub, a male, seemed to be growing particularly well, even though – because of its scanty and irregular meals – it was probably not as big as a captive cub would have been at the same age.

Rat-like tooth-marks surrounding the four big punctures in the buffalo's throat showed that the youngsters had started to practise their inherited killing techniques, and no doubt they felt they had earned the right to feed on their prize. Tara, however, did not approve of them being out and about in daylight hours, and suddenly called them from across the river, The elder female, who happened to be eating at that moment, looked up at the summons and flicked her tail a couple of times before running off in the direction of the call. No hungry human child, I felt sure, would have been half so obedient!

Though always lagging behind the other two in physical

development, the weak cub continued to make better progress, and one night in December she unconsciously gave some visitors an object lesson in family behaviour. That evening at sunset I took a party of guests to the Double-Storey Machan where, on the site across the river, the tigers had killed and half-eaten a buffalo the night before. Just before dark Tara's Male appeared: as he turned his great head towards the machan, his eyes blazed back the last afterglow of day. When he had begun to feed, I gradually turned on the red lamp in the tree above so that we could continue to watch him.

A few minutes after dark a much smaller figure materialised out of the darkness: the third cub, which lay down, front paws together, at a respectful distance while her father got on with his meal, tail-on to her. For a while he did not appear to acknowledge her presence. Then he got up, turned to her briefly as if to say 'Your turn now', and moved off into the night – whereupon the scraggy daughter, only one-fifth his size, took over the kill. Later in the night, after she had eaten her fill, he returned for a second helping.

Where was the 'ineffable malignity' of the Victorian writers? Where the 'embodiment of devilish cruelty'? With that one charming display of manners Tara's Male showed what calumny had been levelled against his kind.

I have now spent hundreds of hours at night watching and listening to the various tigers on their kills; and often, as I have walked home alone, they have seen or heard me pass – a fact confirmed by the morning's study of tracks. Never once have they reacted aggressively – for well-fed tigers are perfectly tranquil.

From watching Tara, her mate and their cubs on kills, I have acquired many rewarding insights into tiger family life. Unlike the lion, whose society is governed by a spirit of competition, and thus presents a primordial comparison with the basics of human society, the tiger appears to be guided by true parental instincts. Far from being a menace to his offspring, the father is remarkably attentive to their welfare: he will feed with them, kill for them in times of scarcity, and allow them to accompany him on quests. It is therefore a remarkable biological fallacy to assume that the male will devour his own offspring.

The tigress, equally, is an exemplary parent. Apart from fulfilling maternal functions, she will yield priority to her cubs in feeding, even if she herself is hungry, and will carry kills to them if they do not accompany her to the kill-site. Young mothers are supposed to be flighty, but Tara's concern for her cubs was touching to see, and they in turn were deeply attached to her.

At the age of fourteen months the male and the elder female cubs started to show signs of independence. Though they still visited the kill-site, it was evident from the alarm calls of hog deer around Tiger Haven that they had begun hunting on their own. (I could tell it was the cubs at work, for in a prime area of this kind full-grown tigers prefer to hunt larger prey such as chital or swamp deer.) The young male especially took to staying away from the communal site.

The weak female, who still appaeared to be physically retarded, always came to the kill in the company of one parent, although, after feeding, she might well leave with the other one. She was also very vocal, and after she had left would call frequently to keep in touch.

In all my hours of observation, I have never seen more than one adult tiger feeding on a kill at once (cubs are another matter). Yet every morning there was fresh evidence of the fact that tiger protocol is based on respect for each other's space and on the premise that all have to feed: numerous resting-places showed where individuals had lain down waiting for their turn to feed – again in strong contrast with the habits of lions, who feed together in a crowd. The incident I mentioned above, when the father gave way to his scrawny daughter, illustrated the principle perfectly: obviously in such circumstances sheer size and the balance of power are temporarily forgotten – though of course a lot depends on how much there is to eat.

In the Kanha National Park Schaller found that the male cub of his study-family was killing almost as effectively as his mother by the age of sixteen months. In Dudhwa, judging by his frequent absences from the kill-site, I reckoned that Tara's male cub was feeding himself fairly adequately at fourteen months: although he knew that food was generally available, he would often disappear for days on expeditions of his own.

One night in early February he attacked a bait in the typical style of a young tiger tackling prey out of its class: he was unable to subdue the animal, and abandoned his attack after scratching and biting it. Later Tara came over the Leopard Bridge and killed the buffalo expertly. Two months later, when the cub was twenty months old, he managed to kill a full-grown buffalo by attacking it from the rear; soon, as his self-confidence grew, he would be killing in orthodox style.

The weakling cub was far slower to mature: though now in good condition, she looked smaller than her brother and sister, and at twenty months she was appreciably smaller than Tara had been at the same age. I wondered if there was some biological explanation for her backwardness. Tara evidently sensed it and was especially solicitous: aware of the cub's tendency to appear at the kill-site earlier than the others, she would try to ensure that there were no trespassers on the scene to block the weakling's chances of an early meal.

Now, as I write in the early spring of 1984, Tara is well and truly established as a wild tigress. She is neither dead nor a man-eater. She is now nearly eight, and if all goes well she should live to about fifteen. For better or for worse – and I am convinced it is for better – her genes are inextricably mingled with those of the other tigers in the Park, and her descendants will tenant Dudhwa for generations to come.

Before the coming of the rains in 1983 I had to change the baiting site, for the committee appointed to report on the man-eating problem had laid down, among other things, that there should be no baiting in the Dudhwa Park or its precincts. This was a thoroughly regressive decision, for the outbreak of man-eating had been caused (as I have explained) by a shortage of prey species, and the ban on baiting merely meant that the wildlife managers were deprived of one effective means of weaning tigers from dependence on an unnatural prey species – man – to which they had been driven by stress of circumstances.

For me, the ban also contained a personal message: it was undoubtedly an attempt by the Director of Project Tiger (who was also secretary of the committee) to restrict my own investigations into tiger behaviour. My own baiting programme had not only helped Tara rear her cubs, but had stopped them straying into a neighbouring range where the Forest Department was trying to catch alleged man-eaters and consign them to slow deaths in zoos. Another worry to me was that although the Government had accepted the principle of paying compensation for humans and domestic stock killed by tigers outside the Park, disbursement of the money was so slow that local people had taken to poisoning tiger kills as a form of retaliation. It was therefore all the more important for me to keep my own tigers in their home range, and I considered myself fully justified in setting up a new site on my own land, which adjoins the Park, and on which this edict does not apply.

The new site was on an open patch of ground where the Soheli river swings in a loop before joining the Neora – an oblong, oval glade some 200 yards long, with a clear patch in the centre flanked by dense grassland. Here, as the summer rains came and went, I maintained a modified programme of baiting with buffaloes, just enough to keep the tiger family from establishing a core area outside the Tiger Haven range. The family structure, however, was disintegrating, and attendance at the site was sporadic. The Male Cub – by now richly coloured like his father – was killing proficiently. After feeding, each individual would depart separately, while swamp deer and chital hairs in their droppings were proof that they were all existing as separate entities. Yet frequent whistles of alarm from the hog deer in the grassland to the south showed that the young females were still pursuing the smaller deer, not yet having attained their full prey range.

One night the Male Cub killed a buffalo with the regulation throat grip. Later, Tara and the Small Cub arrived and fed with him. Next day, as usual, Jackson covered the remains of the carcass with grass to protect it from vultures, and when, just before dusk, he returned to the site, he found the Male Cub back in occupation. Then the Small Cub arrived, whereupon the elder sibling surprisingly abandoned his kill and went off, returning to feed again only after his sister had eaten her fill. According to Jackson, who had a good view, the Small Cub was quite a bit smaller at twenty-seven months than Tara had been at twenty months. The difference may have been due to the fact that hand-reared animals grow faster than wild ones, with better feeding; or it may merely have been that the Small Cub was physically retarded.

I now had visual proof that the father, mother and elder brother had all abandoned their kills so that the weakling cub could feed. I had witnessed similar concern in Harriet, my she-leopard, who would allow her cubs to feed before her, even if she was hungry, and it occurred to me still more forcibly that the solitary cats are far more solicitous of their young than are lions. For lions, the social stresses of community living mean that their behaviour is governed by considerations of precedence: the stronger animals feed first, and weakling cubs often starve in times of scarcity. Tigers have more sophisticated social arrangements; but I noticed that Tara's family frequently functioned as a pride when they were all together at a kill. One night after they had finished off a carcass, father and son departed separately but later joined up near the Spillway Machan and went off together past Leopard Haven. Intolerance among tigers is triggered by hunger, and by threats to territorial domination; I believe that if prey is plentiful, tigers related to each other, however distantly, are capable of much easier coexistence than has hitherto been thought possible.

One evening I sat on the machan overlooking the new site. The sun, a great ball of fire, was setting behind a sea of grass when I heard a series of fourteen modulated tiger calls from the south. I recognised the voice as Tara's. Then suddenly a falsetto *ah!* floated across the narrow stream – the call of a dependent cub. The sound was repeated six times at short intervals, and I waited expectantly; but dusk was closing in, and objects were scarcely visible when Tara at last appeared on the kill.

By then her cubs were two years and three months old. According to accepted theory, female cubs become independent at the age of two years. It therefore occurred to me that it might be the backwardness of the weakling cub which had stopped Tara coming into season again and having another mating. Zoos claim that tigresses breed first at three and a half to four, and that cubs become independent of their parents at one and a half

Above *Tara's elder daughter with a kill on the river bank*
Below *Tiger etiquette: Tara* (right) *abandons the remains of a kill to her weakling daughter*

to two. I realise that these figures cannot be expected to apply in the wild, since captive animals have no function but to procreate: they do not have to search for prey, and the constant presence of the male in confinement ensures that the female comes into season as soon as possible. Wild tigresses, in contrast, not only have to hunt their food, but also are essentially solitary, and thus seldom in contact with the males, who seek them only when the female's seasonal cycle renders her sexually receptive. The fact remains that Tara first bred at the age of five years and four months.

This fact has made me very sceptical about the great breeding successes claimed by the officials of Project Tiger. Much reliable study has been done of lions, which, living as they do in the open plains, are relatively easy to observe. Qualified scientists such as Schaller, Guggisberg and Bertram have recorded a great deal about their habits and behaviour. The tiger, on the other hand, lives in dense habitat as a solitary individual, and much of our knowledge of his way of life has been gained by inference and conjecture – especially as no scientists have been encouraged to study him by the bureaucrats in charge of his welfare.

For this reason I believe that the population increases claimed in recent years are quite unrealistic. Whereas Schaller established five and a half per cent as the annual rate of increase in the Serengeti National Park of Tanzania, where the lion enjoys the social insurance of pride protection, the officials of Corbett National Park claim an increase in their number of tigers from 44 to 112 in ten years – an impossible fifteen per cent. Still more impossible is their claim of having one tiger to every 4·7 square kilometres. Since euphoric claims of this kind have been accepted internationally as fact, and since successful tiger management has become a status symbol, I believe that a cool, impartial reappraisal is necessary. Local officials vie with one another to produce spectacular increases in numbers – and of course, any figures submitted by bureaucrats must show a steady upward trend: otherwise, those putting in the returns will look inefficient.

Above *The 500lb. cat: Tara's Male with a buffalo*
Below *Tara's Male and his three cubs all feed together: a unique photograph*

The tiger and the lion are biologically similar – the two species have been mated in the Calcutta Zoo to produce an absurd caricature called a Tilitigon – yet ethologically they are quite different. The morning and evening choruses of the lion throw out full-throated promises of violence and unconcealed menace in defence of the pride's open territory, which is continually under pressure from neighbours. The subdued call of the tiger is a spatial warning in a forest habitat, given to ensure the sanctity of individual space.

Thus, although both have the same gestation period and parturition habits, it is clear that the marked differences in social structure and habitat must influence their breeding dynamics. In Africa the open terrain, the abundance and size of prey, the good visibility and the need to consume what is killed at a single sitting because of the competition from scavengers – all these factors have evolved the lion into a communal hunter. The tiger, in contrast, has to depend on smaller prey species, and would starve if he had to share kills with other animals of his kind. Living in the forest, he does not face such great competition from scavengers, and has plenty of cover in which to hide his kills until he has eaten them out. Hence his way of life has evolved him into a solitary cat – of course, with local modifications, as are evident in this narrative.

It is well established that ungulates which live in open plains are much more efficient breeders than solitary animals, due to induced communal receptivity (one female bringing another into season), the ability of the males, which are always around, to serve more than one female, and perhaps to a smaller mortality rate. Lions share several of these advantages. The lionesses come into season simultaneously, and because there are usually several lions to serve them, the cubs are all born at more or less the same time. This is a great social advantage, as one lioness will look after and even suckle the cubs of another that is away hunting. The males – once looked upon as irresponsible freeloaders – actively maintain the sanctity of the pride's area and the security of its members, defending them against the potential aggression of other males.

The tiger has no such social insurance. Once a tigress comes into season, she alternates between periods of extreme restlessness, during which she searches for a male, and periods of remaining static, during which she is receptive. There are many factors against her. The time of her maximum receptivity may not coincide with the presence of a male, and she may have to go through her whole cycle again. Even if she does find a male at the right time, persistent copulation is needed to induce ovulation. Then, once she has mated, she is on her own: although the male will occasionally come to help her, she normally has to find her own prey, which means leaving the cubs for long periods exposed to all kinds of danger. And they will remain dependent on her until able to fend for themselves.

All these factors, reinforced by my own experience with Tara and her family, convince me that the lion has a confirmed reproductive advantage. If wild lions in good conditions achieve only the five and a half per cent increase observed by Schaller over a four-year period, I am certain that tigers must achieve less. Definite figures will never be obtained, but Paul Leyhausen's estimate of a two per cent increase in free-living tigers seems much closer to reality than the fifteen per cent claimed in Corbett National Park.

To return to Tara: during the past few months I have been much struck by the difference in her reaction to me according to whether or not the dependent cub has been with her. If she is alone, and comes across me, she vanishes quickly; but if the cub is present, she feels compelled to adopt a protective attitude and demonstrate against me to cover its retreat.

Thus when I once found her sitting alone in the river, cooling off, she pin-pointed the click of my camera with great accuracy and swiftly moved into cover. Yet a few days later, as I walked along the bank in mid-afternoon, with the sun blazing down and the temperature well over 100 degrees F. in the shade, I caught sight of her sitting next to a horizontal log in the water. Just as I was beginning to wonder why she did not move off, I spotted a small head emerging from under the log, and Tara's expression broadened into a snarl of disapproval at my intrusion. Her explosive growls increased in volume and intensity until the cub thought fit to move away, whereupon the mother also disappeared into cover.

Another scene will always haunt me. One night as I sat on

the Double-Storey Machan I heard a deep, moaning call. Soft, resonant and mysterious, apparently divorced from time and space, the noise seemed to come from nowhere, and its cadence faded away at some indeterminate point. When it came again, it was apparently from a different direction, and sounded equally disembodied. But I recognised the voice as Tara's.

As she called, a peacock roosting in a sal tree began to match her every note with its two-tone alarm signal, and from high up in the canopy a troop of rhesus monkeys started giving throaty alarm-coughs as they gazed down anxiously at the brilliantly-moonlit forest floor. Far off in the plains to the south a hog deer sounded its piping whistle; on the escarpment a muntjac barked. All around me the growing members of the tiger family were seeking their independent ways of existence.

The jungle reveals its secrets only to its votaries, and now, wrapped in a blanket against the chill of night, I was one of them. I sat spellbound by the magic of the moment. Presently Tara ceased to call, and soon the jungle fell silent again. Then – without a sound, apparently from nowhere – a ghostly shape materialised on the far bank of the river. It was the smallest cub, granted free access to the kill by her ever-watchful mother's warning calls, which had cleared the way of possible intruders.

On the morning of March 2, 1984 I got an enormous and immensely welcome surprise. Checking Tara's movements during the previous night, I found that she had visited a kill at the Spillway Site, crossed the river, walked east along the north bank and turned up the earth road which climbs the escarpment opposite the Leopard Bridge. After 400 yards she had left the road, known as Am Danda, and gone into the forest to the east. Then, some time later, she had come back out on to the road *with two small cubs*.

When I saw the tiny pug-marks in some sand at the base of the escarpment, I could hardly believe my eyes. I had not even known that Tara was pregnant, let alone that she had given birth. When her previous family had first appeared, after being weaned at the age of five months, their pugs had been slightly larger than those of Harriet when full grown, but these new ones were minute. Even allowing for the fact that the young of all the great cats start life with oversized feet, I judged that the two newcomers could not have been larger than Tiffany, my fishing cat, and that they were probably about fifteen days old.

It was obvious that Tara had been shifting them for the first time in the automatic safety measure which ensures that cubs do not stay too long in any one place; but – mysteriously – although the small pug-marks appeared again on the Tiger Haven side of the Leopard Bridge, there was none on the bridge itself. The only possible conclusion was that Tara had carried the cubs over the bridge, one by one.

At the Spillway Site the infants had been surprisingly active while their mother fed, and multiple miniature tracks were etched in the sand leading away to the Mating Copse, into which they had followed their mother after she had eaten. I judged that one of the cubs was a male and the other a female, for one pug-mark was narrower, with slimmer toes, than the other. The great pugs of Tara's Male showed that he, too, had later entered the copse.

I was astonished to realise that Tara must have mated at the beginning of the November season: although I had been continuously trying to monitor her movements, I had not had the faintest suspicion that she had been through the mating cycle again. Indeed, I had been disappointed and rather worried that nothing had happened, and I had imagined that the continued dependence of the weakling cub had retarded her return to fertility. And yet, sad as I was to have missed the whole performance – the rolling growls of invitation from the tigress, and the vibrant summons of the possessive male – I was overjoyed that two more infant tigers had arrived, to help ensure that their noble species may survive into the future.

15

THE WAY AHEAD

Somehow the priorities of our conservation programme have become hopelessly muddled: the whole effort has got bogged down in political and parochial bickering. Wildlife is essentially an international subject. Migratory birds, for instance, pass through many countries, and India can do nothing to stop the slaughter of Siberian cranes in Iran, Afghanistan or Pakistan. A tigress was found with her head shattered by a bomb which someone had placed in her kill. No inquiry was possible because she had come from Nepal and died in the Indian border area.

Yet – the world being governed by humans – the administration of wildlife funds and the management of wildlife programmes inevitably devolve on national organisations and become subject to national restraints. The developed countries generously gave a great deal of money to save the tiger, but in India we claim Project Tiger as an Indian venture. Not only that: we have given over most of its administration to the various State governments, all of which are under strong political and financial pressures. Although Project Tiger still falls within the central sector, the Government of India has unilaterally committed the States to producing half the funds needed, and this they greatly resent, claiming that their budgets are not large enough even for ever-increasing human needs, so they cannot afford the luxury of preserving animals.

In a democracy wild animals cannot exist without the will of the people. Unless the people living on the periphery of a wildlife park derive some benefit from it, the park cannot exist successfully for long. At the moment locals do derive benefit, in the form of firewood and grass for thatching, but they also suffer considerable aggravation from wild animals, and even though compensation is now payable on domestic stock taken by tigers, it is often not available unless a subvention is paid to the official who assesses the claim.

One of the greatest difficulties is that the Forest Department is a commercial organisation, charged with producing revenue. Yet by historical accident and administrative convenience it also has charge of wildlife. In the old days the two sides of the business ran easily in harness: the British administrators regarded the animals of the forest as a valuable source of recreation, and culled and conserved them accordingly. Today, however, the demands of forestry and wildlife pull in opposite directions, for by the Indian Wildlife Act of 1972 commercial exploitation is banned from any area designated as a wildlife reserve. Thus it is in the interest of the Forest Department to keep wildlife parks as small as possible, and officials naturally resist any attempt at expansion. The result is that most tiger reserves are no more than islands of conservation under siege by the human invader, and too small to carry a tiger population which will be genetically viable in the long run.

It is now clear that commercial forestry and wildlife management are mutually antagonistic. Every tree felled for money or for forestry management means the destruction of habitat for birds, insects, reptiles and small mammals. A clean forest floor, on which humans scavenge the remnants of fallen trees, is anathema to the wildlife manager, for the presence of humans in the forest inevitably disturbs the animals and leads to fires which devastate vast areas. The planting of quick-growing, exotic species such as eucalyptus is equally inimical to wildlife, for it produces no under-storey of shrubs and grasses on which ungulates can feed, or in which predators can find shelter.

For these reasons, commercial forestry and wildlife management should obviously be run by separate administrations, each with its own expertise and training schemes. In the past the scientifically-trained forester looked on wildlife as a kind of bonus, in the form of the sport provided by shooting; now, when he is called on to act as a wildlife manager, he simply does not have the requisite knowledge and training. He becomes an 'expert' simply through holding a certain rank, and for his knowledge he is forced to rely largely on outdated books written by hunters whose view of animals was hopelessly distorted by the fact that they were always trying to kill them, and that the animals' behaviour was altered by continuous pursuit. At the same time, to be involved with wildlife has become a status-symbol, and attracts an unhealthy amount of kudos.

What India needs is an equivalent of the United States's Fish and Wildlife Service – a specialist Government body, with its own scientific expertise. Instead, we have left the care of our wildlife in the hands of a commercial organisation whose political masters are constantly demanding increases in revenue, as well as privileges for the voters on whom they depend to keep them in office. It is sometimes said that, but for the Forest Department, there would be no wildlife left; in fact it is a wonder that there is anything left *in spite of* the Department.

A specialist Wildlife Department would be able to work out what the minimum population of tigers in any one pool should be. The I.U.C.N., as I have said, laid down a figure of 300; yet the fact is that most Indian reserves, as they now stand, do not have room for even half that number of tigers. A pool of 300 tigers would demand a minimum habitat area of between 2,000 and 3,000 square miles, and reserves that size are available nowhere in India – although the Sunderbans and Manas would qualify, if suitable extra areas could be added. (For comparison, the Tsavo National Park in Kenya covers 8,000 square miles, the Corbett National Park 225, Dudhwa 190.)

What is certain is that in any finite area there are limits beyond which the tiger population cannot increase. The great predators are essentially territorial animals, and although they show a good deal of tolerance if prey is plentiful, they cannot stand becoming overcrowded. It this happens, they automatically adjust their numbers, either by the superfluous animals moving out into other ranges (if this is possible), or by the tigresses curtailing their own breeding-rate.

In the twelve years since the inception of Project Tiger, we have seen a welcome increase in numbers – although it is hard to tell how much of the gain is real and how much theoretical. Bureaucracy requires that the number of tigers in any one reserve rises steadily from year to year, thus demonstrating the success and skill of the local administration. If the return for one year shows forty tigers, the next will probably show forty-five, the next fifty-one, and so on. Real numbers, however, may be very different. Thus the present official estimate for the Corbett National Park is 103, but people outside the bureaucracy say that the reserve contains no more than forty. In Simlipal the official total is sixty-one, the unofficial estimate – given by another forester – between six and eight.

Whatever the true gain, it may turn out to be no more than temporary, for the small pools of tigers which we have managed to save will inevitably run the risk of deterioration from inbreeding, unless we can substantially increase the space available to them, or link existing areas by forest corridors, so that the tigers can effect genetic exchanges on their own. The very least we must do is build up a body of expertise at darting and translocation, so that if all else fails tigers can be efficiently sedated and transferred from one reserve to another.

We do, however, need to think bigger than this. We need to accept the principle of complete environmental protection, with the tiger – our national animal – as a symbol of the apex of the biotic pyramid. We need to make wildlife reserves inviolate and free from all commercial intrusion by man. Above all, we need to think more in international terms – not only for fund-raising, but for the creation of bigger reserves. One International Biosphere Reserve, for example, could be created by uniting the present forests of Bahraich, Kheri and Pilibhit with those of Suklaphanta and Bardia in Nepal, taking in all the intermediate areas of human population. The problems would be formidable, I know; but I repeat that they must be tackled with imagination.

Above all, we must act with *emotion*. Wildlife can only be

saved now by a crusade, and like all crusades this one must have an emotional appeal. For too long the tiger has been looked after (if that is the word) by the bureaucrat with one eye on the politician, and the politician with one eye on the main chance. The rigid scientific attitude which frowns on an intermixing of sub-species is no longer adequate; rather, we must respond with open hearts and enthusiasm.

I believe that we have an inherited duty to preserve all animals. If something has come down to us in nature, through evolution or the Almighty – whatever your faith may be – I am convinced that we should accept it and look after it. Just because a creature is of little material use to us, and does us no immediately obvious practical good, we have no right to let its kind die out.

If we consider ourselves as trustees of the planet, we must mend our ways and cherish everything we have left. Our insensate plunder of the environment has brought disaster on every front. Destruction of the forests has led to soil erosion in the hills and flooding in rivers lower down. Extensive quarrying has caused hillsides to collapse. Even the climate seems to have changed for the worse under man's baleful influence. Through persecution and negligence, we all-but exterminated the tiger.

Animals should be allowed to live for the sake of evolution, not because of the use they can be to the master race: we must cease to think of them as beasts, and accord them the dignity which we consider essential in dealing with our own kind. Their physical functions, after all, are the same as ours. Not only should we conserve the armadillo, the only animal known to get leprosy; we should protect the badger (even though he is suspected of carrying tuberculosis to domestic stock) and all the other beings, great and small, with whom we share the Earth. Above all we should fight to save the tiger, magnificent king of the predators, and a wonder of creation.

APPENDIX
The Tara Controversy

The controversy that has raged over Tara is one of those bitter and pointless wrangles which break out when a variety of people have conflicting interests in a common object. Some of those who joined in did so for pseudo-scientific or obstructionist reasons. Most people, however, had purely selfish motives, and were trying to score political points or win themselves advancement. Hardly any of them were concerned about the welfare of the tiger, which was what they were supposed to be working for.

I must emphasise once again that my project of attempting to re-introduce a hand-reared tiger to the jungle received the whole-hearted support of the Prime Minister. Even this fundamental fact was later denied. Trouble started even before I left England, when Paul Leyhausen, Chairman of the I.U.C.N.'s Cat Group, took it upon himself to announce that no European zoo had pure-bred Indian tigers. It was this remark, repeated to a wildlife functionary in India, which triggered the ominous telephone call from Delhi, which I received in England, asking me not to bring a tigress of doubtful lineage into the country.

It seemed ironic that Leyhausen, who now proclaimed the need to maintain genetic purity, had also laid down that the minimum number of tigers needed to maintain genetic diversity in any self-contained pool was *no fewer than* 300. Since — as he well knew — none of India's reserves contained a population of anything like that size, he was in effect saying that every group of tigers which survived in our wildlife reserves was condemned to inbreeding. By his standards, the number in the Dudhwa National Park —

fifty at the most — was hopelessly small, and would guarantee sterility or at least deterioration in a few generations.

In any case I ignored the telephone call and set out with Tara on our great journey. The fact that the cub was detained for fifteen days in Customs Bond at Delhi Zoo had nothing to do with scientific objections to her arrival; it was simply typical Indian bureaucracy. When in the end she was issued with an import certificate, the substantial duty was waived — again showing that the project had the approval of the Government of India.

At home in Kheri the atmosphere was at first equally cordial. Before my trip to England the Chief Wildlife Warden of the State had been most enthusiastic about my project, and had gone so far as to suggest that I should try to bring back a second cub so that the Forest Department could try a rehabilitation project of their own. When he saw my quizzical expression he no doubt concluded — quite rightly — that I was thinking of the miserable failure the Department had had in trying to reintroduce the Indian lion into the Chandraprabha sanctuary, and he hastened to add that he would ask me to take overall charge of the scheme. Luckily nothing came of this suggestion.

When I brought Tara to Tiger Haven, my relations with the Forest Department were still most amicable, and for a while the young tigress was looked upon as the showpiece of the Park. Press correspondents and photographers came in droves to see her, and much sentimental mush was published about 'filial relationships', as if she were an adopted daughter, in describing what, to me, was a deeply serious endeavour. The Park Director, R. L. Singh, who fancied himself as a popular author, wrote a number of articles about the project for Hindi newspapers.

All went well until March 1977 when, in the national elections, Mrs Gandhi's Government fell. No longer could the managers of wildlife projects expect the degree of support that they had enjoyed as a result of Mrs Gandhi's personal interest.

Even so, Tara's upbringing continued unopposed until the outbreak of man-eating began at Sathiana. To people ignorant of local detail, it no doubt seemed plausible to say that the man-eater must be Tara, whose early life among humans had (it was claimed) deprived her of a tiger's normal responses. This, as I have explained, bore no relation to the fact; yet the succession of events was sufficiently striking for a biased person to make capital from the claim that all these killings were due to the release of Tara. In time, however, the first outcry died down.

The first serious opposition came in 1979, when I submitted a paper to the International Tiger Symposium in Delhi, claiming that I had success-fully introduced a zoo-bred tigress to the wild. This was too much for many leading officials of Project Tiger, who all declared that such a feat was impossible, and it also provoked Professor Leyhausen to take further action. This time he acted as a member of a separate wildlife body, the Survival

Services Commission, and persuaded its chairman, Sir Peter Scott, to write me a personal letter. This said that the Steering Committee of the Commission understood that the tigress supplied to me by Twycross Zoo was a hybrid of two sub-species, and therefore I should make sure she did not breed, thereby producing another 'genetic cocktail'. Having given this extra stir to the storm in the gene cup, the fearless Cat Chairman resigned.

The request was utterly unrealistic. Tara by then had been living wild for months, beyond the control of any human, and it would have been impossible for anyone but me (or perhaps Jackson) either to find her or identify her correctly. She was selecting her own partners in the jungle and could, in theory, already have become pregnant by a wild tiger. I hardly need say that I ignored the instructions.

The Forest Department, who had always maintained that the rehabilit-ation of hand-reared carnivores was impossible, retaliated to my success in a quite different way. When the Median Tigress had to be shot at Dudhwa in November 1980, they stated categorically that the dead man-eater was Tara, thus neatly proving their own thesis that a hand-reared carnivore, not having learnt a proper killing technique from its parents, must turn to hunting humans, the easiest form of prey.

It was biologically impossible that the man-eater could have been Tara, for the dead tigress had been accompanied by a cub more than two years old, and Tara was much too young to have produced such a grown-up depend-ant. The Department ignored this awkward fact. Another slight problem they had was to explain how my tigress — unable by their account to kill normal prey — had managed to survive for two years and ten months in the wild. This difficulty they solved by unscrupulously announcing that twenty-two human kills spread over the past two years had all been Tara's work — even though Government statistics established that the kills had been the work of two males. What had kept her going, by their account, was one human being about every five weeks.

The whole claim was obvious nonsense; such rubbish, in fact, that I was amazed to hear it put forward by people in positions of authority. Yet this was nothing compared with the contortions of fact and fiction in which the Department officials later found themselves entwined.

It was most unfortunate that I should fall foul of Project Tiger since they — in theory, at any rate — were working for the same ultimate cause as I was. Yet perhaps a clash was unavoidable, for S. R. Choudhury, one of the Field Directors, and a presumptive heir to the post of Director, had acquired a wild tigress cub called Khairi some time before I got Tara, and had brought her up in a constant blaze of publicity, saying that she too would be returned to the wild.

Khairi was found as a tiny cub on the bank of a river from which she took her name: her mother demonstrated against a party of villagers, but when they shouted at her she ran away and abandoned her infant. Choudhury, who was Field Director for the Simlipal Reserve, therefore brought her up — and gained a great deal of kudos for his handling of a supposedly ferocious animal.

The cause of his clash with me was my statement that by the age of twenty months Tara's urge to return to her kind was beyond the control of any human being. Choudhury denied that this could be correct, and cited the behaviour of his own tigress to prove it. Though older than Tara, Khairi was still amenable and docile.

That much was true. The greater truth which the argument concealed was that Khairi's upbringing and treatment had been entirely different from Tara's. Whereas I lived on the very edge of the jungle, and constantly took Tara into the forest, Choudhury lived at Jashipur, some thirty miles from the nearest point of the Simlipal reserve, and there he kept Khairi more or less as a household pet. He did take her to the jungle twice, but only for brief periods; the natural urge which pulled Tara inexorably back to nature was controlled in Khairi by the regular administration of anti-oestrogen tablets. These made her not only docile, but also extremely fat: she was the flabbiest tiger I have ever seen, and it was manifestly the drugs which suppressed her natural instincts.

Nevertheless, Choudhury doted on her, and she won him wide renown. Later she attracted a great deal of gossip as well, for it was said that funds earmarked for Project Tiger were diverted to her benefit. Foresters and wildlife guards, who were supposed to patrol the core area of the Simlipal Reserve and keep out poachers, were deputed to look after her and monitor her every movement: if she scratched herself ninety-nine times a day, a note was made of it. Inevitably, she remained a house pet, imprinted on her human captors, and subject to meaningless, pseudo-scientific observation. When she died in April 1980, her poor owner was so heartbroken that he himself expired a few months later, but not before he had launched an entirely unprovoked attack on me and my project.

In 1979 he was appointed to lead an official inquiry into the man-eating problem, and a year later he published a report. In this he did at least exonerate Tara by recording that all the convicted man-eaters to date had proved to be males; but he also came out with the gratuitous statement that Tara had 'apparently been naturally eliminated', and that 'no super-predator can be rehabilitated'. At no stage of his inquiries did he consult me to find out the facts.

Meanwhile I had — perhaps injudiciously — criticised the international tiger symposium of 1979 as an exercise in self-advertisement, for some of the Project officials had submitted as many as five or six papers each. I should therefore have been prepared for the closing-of-ranks with which the Department met my jibe — for the officials of Project Tiger had been recruited from among them.

The next assault, in 1981, took the form of a series of letters from the

Director of the Project, who wrote to say that he now had conclusive proof that Tara had been of mixed parentage, and that she should not therefore have been released into the Indian forests, as her arrival amounted to genetic pollution. This was followed by high-flown sentiments about the 'pious onus on conservationists' to maintain the breeding integrity of the Indian tiger, and the 'untoward consequences' likely to follow from the rehabilitation of a racially-impure animal.

To this argument I replied that such a dogmatic approach might possibly be acceptable if we had viable breeding stocks of tigers, but that if we applied it to an endangered species, without a sound breeding nucleus anywhere, we should only encourage inbreeding and an ultimate deterioration of our entire remaining population. I added that although the main aim of my project had been to demonstrate the feasibility of returning a hand-reared cub to the wild, I did not believe it mattered if a slightly alien sub-species *had* been introduced: one animal's genes would soon be absorbed in a population of over fifty. The origin of the species as a whole is acknowledged to be Siberia, and the differences in the size and colouring of present-day tigers are due to the influence of varied climates and habitats over a long period.

The second point brought up by the Director was that the reintroduction of any great cat is hazardous to humans. His argument was well reasoned, and no doubt sounded convincing when read out in a city office. In the jungle, however, it was divorced from reality.

The argument ran as follows. A captive-reared carnivore inevitably learns to depend for food on the person bringing it up, and this results in the development of a tiger that does not fear man. Such an animal will have a tendency to re-visit the place of its upbringing, and may well go up to a person in search of food. The natural reaction of a man approached by a tiger is to run, which awakes the attack instinct in the tiger, and may result in the mauling and killing of the man.

To someone without practical experience, this might make sense, but in fact the argument is riddled with fallacies. The central one is to say that when an animal has opted for the wild, it may go up to humans in search of food. This does not happen. Both Prince and Tara had shown me that the solitary cats, if brought up in a suitable environment, become uncontrollable in their desire to return to their own species, and in any case they recognise not species, but individuals. This was clearly shown by Prince, who knew Eelie and played with her, but instantly chased her son with deadly intent, even though the young dog closely resembled its mother. Once a great cat has made the transition to the completely different surroundings of the night-time jungle, it develops the same instinctive avoidance of man as its wild counterparts. Man, by his very mode of life, is a stranger to the animals of the forest, who instinctively shun the unfamiliar: it is this fact that has saved him from being accepted as a prey species.

This was made clear by the behaviour of both Prince and Tara, who occasionally came back to Tiger Haven, but never approached any human, not even the one on whom they had depended. I also recalled the time when Prince, still dependent on me for food and company, was living at Leopard Haven, and a gang of contractors' men came to ply the river for driftwood. For fifteen days the men were working right in the centre of his range, yet none of them once set eyes on him. Hungry as he was, he did not go up to them.

On the subject of instinct, I pointed out that the inherited instinct to hunt does not require a course of instruction from parents: it is there already, and a young carnivore needs only the hunger-imperative, maturity, and experience to evolve into a complete predator. I cited the instance of Tiffany, my fishing cat, rescued from a forest fire when she was a week old and then bottle-fed at Tiger Haven, whom we found a month later in a shallow stream, dabbling with her paws for fish. No mother had taught her where her food would come from – and yet she knew. I also gave the example of Tara's cubs, at the age of nine months, joining their father in an attack on a tied-up bait, and going for the throat in an instinctive death-grip.

All this was hard, practical fact, gained from innumerable hours of fieldwork. Yet it made no impression on the walls of dogma which defend the Headquarters of Project Tiger from any information which the inmates do not find palatable. The Director reverted to the question of genetic pollution, and stated that in the interests of heredity Tara – supposing she was still alive – and/or her cubs would have to be destroyed.

While the argument was in progress, the Director of the Dudhwa Park, R. L. Singh, had been making great capital out of the fact that he had shot the 'polluted' tigress when she turned man-eater, and now he claimed he had drawn her two cubs into a particular area by baiting, so that he could eliminate them too. He appeared unruffled by the fact that the tiger which he claimed was a double hybrid looked to be between eight and ten years old, whereas Tara, supposedly his mother, was still not even six.

As the man-eating problem became inextricably mixed up with the Tara controversy, I must refer to it here again. In February 1981, when sixty people had already been killed in Kheri, I suggested at a meeting of the Indian Board for Wildlife, held in Delhi under the Chairmanship of the Prime Minister, Mrs Gandhi, that a committee should be formed immediately to investigate the cause of the phenomenon and suggest remedies. The idea was accepted: a committee was set up, with the Director of Project Tiger as its Secretary; but besides being required to report on man-eaters, the body was given an additional mandate to report on the feasibility of introducing hand-reared predators into the wild. In my opinion the two issues should never have been linked, as one had no connection with the other, and were combined merely to keep me out of the committee.

A year later the Committee published a lengthy report, in which it stressed — quite rightly — that the main reason for the outbreak of man-eating had been the pressure of human population on tiger habitat. But in the second part of their reference — on which they had not seen fit to consult me — they briefly emphasised that the return of hand-reared carnivores to the wild was impossible. Since the same arguments appeared, word for word, as the Director had used in his letters to me, it was clear that he had written the report as well. Yet there was one significant departure from his previous position.

Earlier, he had stated that he was not convinced either by the Park Director's claim that the man-eater he had shot was Tara, or by my claim that Tara was established in the wild. Now the Committee supported my earlier contention that the facial markings of the shot man-eater did not tally with those shown in pictures of Tara when she was still growing up. In other words, they agreed that it was not Tara who had been shot at Dudhwa. Yet it is easy to see that they *had* to agree this; for to agree that it was she who died then would have been tantamount to admitting that she had lived for two years and ten months in the wild — from January 1978 to November 1980 — before suddenly turning compulsive man-eater and killing five people. With such an admission, their dogma about hand-reared predators being unable to survive in the jungle would have gone up in flames.

The Park Director had already sought to solve this tricky problem by the statement that during the interim period Tara had eked out a living by killing twenty-two humans; but this had been disproved and the Committee's conclusions now ran as follows:

1 The facial markings of the shot tigress were not the same as Tara's. Therefore it was not Tara who had been killed.

2 At the same time, there was no trace of Tara to show that she was still alive.

3 There was, however, a distinct resemblance between the shot man-eater and the tigress which I had photographed on a kill in April 1980 and had claimed to be Tara living wild.

4 It was this animal, a kind of pseudo-Tara, which had turned man-eater and had been shot at Dudhwa in November 1980.

Thus, by pretending that Tara did not exist any more, the Committee solved the problems of genetic pollution and absolved themselves from the need to eliminate any more tigers on the supposition that they might be Tara's cubs. Their conclusion also dismissed my whole experiment in rehabilitation as a failure. They did not seek my views at any stage of their inquiry, nor ask for any evidence which I could have given them.

The report was submitted to the Steering Committee of Project Tiger and released to the Press, but no copy was sent to me, although I and my projects were freely criticised, and I had to sneak a preview. When I saw what the report contained, I wrote to the Prime Minister in her capacity as Chairman of the Indian Board for Wildlife (of which I am a member), asking her to place my version of the facts before the Board when it convened for its annual meeting. I listed my points of disagreement with the Committee, which I accused of prejudice.

The Chairman, however, did not think it appropriate to place my letter before the Board, but referred it back to the same Committee. I retorted that I did not expect the authors of the report to withdraw such definitely-expressed views, and I asked to appear before the Steering Committee of Project Tiger, of which Mrs Gandhi is also Chairman.

Seven months later, before this last request had been refused or granted, I was asked by the Man-Eater Committee to meet them in Delhi. The Director of Project Tiger's first words were that we should forget past events and work together for the future: I said I agreed entirely, and hoped that we could start with a clean slate.

Yet it soon became apparent that he was prepared to make peace only on his own terms, and that he did not intend to retract any of his earlier claims. Having based his 'certain recognition' of the various tigresses on their facial markings, he now refused to see what to me were obvious resemblances between Tara and the tigress whom I photographed on the kill at night.

The Director also shifted the basis of recognition to stripe-patterns, which according to him, remain constant throughout life. Now the recognition of tigers by their stripe-patterns is an empirical science, and has been employed in India only since Schaller used it as a means of distinguishing various tigers from each other over a relatively short period. No one had made a long-term study of how the patterns change during an animal's life, and the Director's confident assertion certainly needs qualification.

My own experience leads me to believe that stripe-patterns naturally alter with every variation in body-size. The skin of the big cats is so loose that the slightest change in posture, or the angle from which they are being observed, produces an apparent difference in the pattern. Even a full belly seems to give new effects. Changes also obviously occur as a young animal puts on bulk and fills out its frame. Again, night photography produces shadows and angles which can elongate or foreshorten some of the stripes. All this shows that stripes cannot be used as an infallible means of recognition.

Nor, for that matter, can face-markings, since these too are liable to change as an animal grows up. Tara's left cheek-stripe (in the form of a catapult) and eye-spot pattern have remained the same as they were when she was growing up at Tiger Haven; so has the unique triangle of stripes on her left hind leg. Yet her right cheek-stripe has changed somewhat, and former projections near the muzzle have coalesced to form a continuous catapult. Also, the half-moon above the right eye has changed position slightly, and the eye-spots and cheek-stripes which were asymmetrical in her early days are now almost even. Similar changes occur in many tigers — yet it is useless to try to explain the process to the Forest Department.

As I feared, our argument proved inconclusive, and the dispute was left unresolved, with the wholly false findings of the report unwithdrawn.

The episode seems to me to symbolise what has gone wrong with the management of wildlife in India today. Instead of accepting what I had done in a practical and creative spirit, the officials of Project Tiger were driven by their own scientific dogma — perhaps also by baser influences such as jealousy — to refute the existence of a unique animal, to deny that anything had been achieved at all, and to erect in their own defence a tissue of counter-claims about as strong as a spider's web.

There is no doubt that at one stage they were definitely in favour of further attempts at reintroduction. When, in the 1970s, the Swedish conservationist Jan Lindblad asked for permission to import two tigresses into India, both the Director of Project Tiger, and Fateh Singh, the Field Director for Ranthambore, were very encouraging. Lindblad began making preparations, but then the Tara controversy erupted, and he was abruptly informed that as hand-reared predators were liable to turn man-eater, as Tara had, he would not get permission after all.

Equally clear is the fact that the climate of opinion, and the apparent problems, have changed a great deal between 1976, when the Tara project was first mooted, and today. Then, it was by no means clear that enough tigers had survived into the era of protection for the species to have a real chance of sustaining itself. Everyone was in favour of trying to swell the slender population by the rehabilitation of a hand-reared cub. Eight years later, with tigers breeding well, it is clear that they will survive if we can only find room for them to maintain their genetic strength.

GLOSSARY

of Principal Animals, Birds and Reptiles

ASIAN ELEPHANT (*Elephas maximus*) More compact than the African elephant. Most tractable. Famous for its services to mankind.

BLACK BUCK (*Antelopa cervicapra*) Handsome antelope on the verge of extinction.

CHITAL (*Axis axis*) Strongly spotted deer, weighing up to 200 lbs. Favourite prey of leopard.

GAVIAL (*Gavialis gangeticus*) Also known as the gharial. The most seriously endangered of India's crocodiles. Protected since 1972.

FISHING CAT (*Felis viverrina*) Rare overall, but fairly common in the Dudhwa area.

GREY LANGUR (*Presbytis entellus*) Long-tailed monkey, up to 40 lbs.

HOG DEER (*Axis porcinus*) Solid-looking, short-legged deer. Up to 125 lb.

INDIAN MONGOOSE (*Herpestes griseus*) A great killer of snakes and rats.

INDIAN TIGER (*Panthera tigris tigris*) One of the seven sub-species of tiger which survive in the world. Some 2,000 now live

213

in India's parks and reserves, where they are fully protected.

JACKAL (*Canis aureus*) Fox-sized predator, common in Dudhwa.

LAMMERGEIER (*Gypaetus barbatus*) Bearded vulture, with wing-span up to ten feet.

LEOPARD (*Panthera pardus*) Three sub-species of leopard survive in India. All are now protected, but numbers have decreased alarmingly.

MARSH CROCODILE (*Crocodylus palustris*) An endangered species which has disappeared from most of India. Also known as the mugger. Now legally protected, but still subject to poaching for its skin.

MONITOR LIZARD (*Varanus monitor*) Agile lizard up to five feet long.

MUNTJAC (*Muntiacus muntjac*) Barking deer, also known as the kakar. Up to 40 lbs.

NILGAI (*Boselaphus tragocamelus*) Large, ungainly antelope which inhabits open plains.

PEACOCK (*Pavo cristatus*) The national bird of India.

PORCUPINE (*Hystrix indica*) Preyed on by tigers and leopards. Up to 40 lbs.

PYTHON (*Python molorus*) Large snake fairly common in Dudhwa.

RHESUS MONKEY (*Macaca mulatta*) Favourite prey species of leopards. Up to 30 lbs.

SAMBAR (*Cervus unicolor*) The largest deer in India. Up to 700 lbs.

SLOTH BEAR (*Melursus ursinus*) Partially protected in India, Nepal and Sri Lanka, but still endangered.

SMOOTH INDIAN OTTER (*Lutra perspicillata*) Fairly common in Dudhwa.

SWAMP DEER (*Cervus duvauceli*) An endangered species, now protected. The Dudhwa National Park is one of its main strongholds in Northern India. Weighs up to 500 lbs.

WILD BOAR (*Sus scrofa*) Favourite prey of the tiger.

WOLF (*Canis lupus*) Partially protected in India since 1972.

ACKNOWLEDGMENTS

I owe an immense debt of gratitude to Tara, the zoo-born tigress who completed the transition from hand-reared status to that of complete independence without untoward incident. That such a historic changeover took place, despite the human pressures which were deliberately built up against the experiment, in spite of the lack of co-operation from the local forest department, and in the face of popular opposition, is a tribute to the non-aggressive reactions of the supreme predator.

My grateful thanks are due to my sister-in-law Mira, who has so painstakingly typed the manuscript, and to Sarah Giles, who handled many of the photographs. I should also like to express my appreciation to John Aspinall for his foreword and for his unfailing moral and material support in the defence of noble animals. Though the human world stands divided, there is neither East nor West for natural creations.

ARJAN SINGH
Dudhwa, January 1984

PHOTOGRAPH CREDITS

The author and publishers are grateful to the following for permission to reproduce colour and black and white photographs: Stanley Breeden, opposite p. 80, between pp. 80–1 (left, above and below); the British Library, opposite p. 33 (below), opposite p. 64 (above and below), opposite p. 65 (below); Lord Glendevon, opposite p. 65 (left); Masahiro Iijima, opposite p. 192 (below); Dieter and Mary Plage, between pp. 80–1 (right, above); Arjan Singh, opposite p. 80 (above and below), between pp. 80–1 (right, below), opposite p. 96, opposite p. 97 (above), opposite p. 128 (below), opposite p. 129 (below), opposite p. 144 (below), between pp. 144–5 (left and right), opposite p. 145 (above and below), opposite p. 160, opposite p. 161 (above and below), opposite p. 192 (above); opposite p. 193 (above and below); Ashok Singh, opposite p. 144 (above); Brijendra Singh, opposite p. 32; S. G. Sommers, opposite p. 97 (below); Hashim Tyabjee, opposite p. 128 (above).

BIBLIOGRAPHY

Brander, A. A. Dunbar, *Wild Animals in Central India*, London, 1923
Brown, J. Moray, *Shikar Sketches*, London, 1887
Campbell, Maj. Walter, *The Old Forest Ranger*, London, 1843
Champion, F.W., *With a Camera in Tigerland*
—— *The Jungle in Sunlight and Shadow*
Corbett, Jim, *Man-Eaters of Kumaon*, New York & Bombay, 1944
—— *The Man-Eating Leopard of Rudraprayag*, London, 1948
—— *The Temple Tiger*, London, 1954
—— *My India*, London, 1952
—— *Jungle Lore*, London & New York, 1953
—— *Tree Tops*, London, 1955
Glasfurd, A.I.R., *Rifle and Romance in the Indian Jungle*, London, 1905
Gordon Cumming, W., *Wild Men and Beasts*, Edinburgh, 1871
Gouldsbury, C.E., *Tigerland*, London, 1913
Inglis, James, *Tent Life in Tigerland*, London, 1888
McDougal, Charles, *The Face of the Tiger*, London, 1977
Mountfort, G., *Saving the Tiger*, London, 1981

Patterson, J.H., *Man-Eaters of Tsavo*, London, 1907

Rice, W., *Tiger Shooting in India*, London, 1857

—— *Indian Game*, London, 1884

Sanderson, G.P., *Thirteen Years among the Wild Beasts of India*, London, 1878

Sankhala, K., *Tiger!*, London, 1978

Schaller, G.B., *The Deer and the Tiger*, Chicago, 1967

—— *The Serengeti Lion*, New York, 1972

Scott, Denton, *The Forests of the Night*

Shakespear, H., *The Wild Sports of India*, London, 1860

Singh, Arjan, *Tiger Haven*, London, 1973

—— *Tara: A Tigress*, London, 1981

—— *Prince of Cats*, London, 1982

Singh, Fateh, Singh, Tejbir & Thapar, Valmik, *Tigers in the Wild*, India, 1983

Smythies, E.A., *Big Game Shooting in Nepal*, Calcutta, 1942

Strachan, A.N., *Mauled by a Tiger*, London, 1933

Williamson, Thomas, *Indian Field Sports*, London, 1807

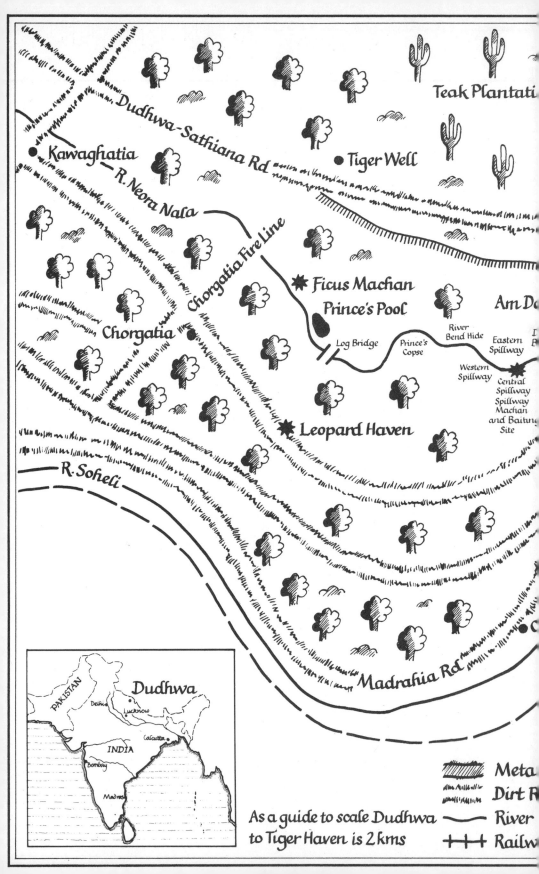